FEAR NOT WARRIOR

Number 75

FEAR NOT WARRIOR
A Study of 'al tîrā' Pericopes in the Hebrew Scriptures

by
Edgar W. Conrad

FEAR NOT WARRIOR
A Study of 'al tîrā' Pericopes in the Hebrew Scriptures

by
Edgar W. Conrad

Scholars Press
Chico, California

FEAR NOT WARRIOR
A Study of 'al tîrā' Pericopes
in the Hebrew Scriptures

by
Edgar W. Conrad

Library of Congress Cataloging in Publication Data

Conrad, Edgar W., 1942–
  Fear not warrior.

  (Brown Judaic studies ; no. 75)
  Includes index.
  1. War—Biblical teaching. 2. Bible. O.T.—Language,
style. I. Title. II. Title: 'Al tîrā' pericopes in the Hebrew
Scriptures. III. Series
BA1199.W2C65   1985   221.6'6   85–10713
ISBN 0–89130–864–4 (alk. paper)
ISBN 0–89130–865–2 (pbk.)

Printed in the United States of America
on acid-free paper

To

VIOLET, AMOS, ETHEL
and in remembrance of
PAUL

Hear, my son, your father's instruction,
    and reject not your mother's teaching;
for they are a fair garland for your head,
    and pendants for your neck.

Prov 1:8

CONTENTS

Page

PREFACE

No book is ever completed without the help and support of friends, and this book is no exception. Professor Bernhard W. Anderson, my former teacher and my friend, has given me constructive insights as he listened to my ideas on "fear not" language during regular Friday luncheons in Princeton during my study leave in 1982. I owe my thanks to my wife Linda who took time out of her own busy research schedule to read the manuscript while in progress. Her suggestions concerning my argument and my writing style has been invaluable. I also owe my thanks to Professor James I. McCord, now president emeritus of Princeton Theological Seminary, whose kind offer of a Visiting Fellowship made it possible to study at Speer Library. Professor Jacob Neusner, who visited Australia in 1983, has been a source of encouragement. His interest in my work was a needed catalyst as it was reaching the "almost but not quite" stage of completion. Finally, I offer my thanks to my colleagues in the department of Studies in Religion at the University of Queensland. They have generated an air of excitement in a young but growing program of religious studies.

Edgar W. Conrad
Brisbane, Queensland
Australia
February 17, 1984

INTRODUCTION

The Aim of the Study

In the Hebrew Scriptures the motif of war is an important component of the conception of the divine. Yahweh himself is identified as a divine warrior (see, e.g., Exod 15:3). In an attempt to understand the significance of the relationship between Yahweh and war many studies have devised methods to get behind the present literary text in a search for origins. Some have looked for those origins in the institution of holy war thought to be characteristic of the so-called Israelite amphictyony[1] while others have sought the origins of Israel's conception of the divine warrior in ancient Near Eastern mythology adapted by Israel.[2] The present study is not a search for the origins of ideas and motifs of war but is an exploration of language associated with war in its present literary setting in the Hebrew Scriptures. The study does not attempt to get behind the text to focus on social institutions or the roots of antecedent ideas. It is concerned rather with the rhetorical features of the text itself and is a systematic examination of certain "fear not" pericopes in the Hebrew Scriptures in order to identify the conventions of "fear not" language associated with war.[3]

The research presented here grows out of my critique of Joachim Begrich's thesis that "fear not" is a central element in the Oracle of Salvation, a genre which he understood as a priestly answer to a distressed individual who came to the temple to offer lament and make petition to Yahweh.[4] Begrich's thesis, which has won a large following among scholars,[5] was based on "fear not" texts in Second Isaiah. I argued that Begrich's study needed to be questioned because he did not take into consideration other "fear not" pericopes in the Hebrew Scriptures as a context for understanding the genre employed in Second Isaiah nor did he consider the rhetorical settings of the genre in the poetry of Second Isaiah.[6] In short, he identified "fear not" pericopes as Oracles of Salvation in Second Isaiah by studying those pericopes in isolation from other possible occurrences of the genre in the Hebrew Scriptures and in isolation from their literary settings in the text of Second Isaiah itself. The present study emerged, then, not because of a prior interest in language associated with war but as an alternative explanation to Begrich's thesis.

1

The study also goes beyond the thesis of Gerhard von Rad, who, in his book, *Der Heilige Krieg im alten Israel,* held that "fear not" was a major motif of the institution of holy war associated with the Israelite amphictyony.[7] It will be maintained that the use of "fear not" in contexts of war is pervasive and cannot be restricted to a pre-monarchic institution. This is particularly the case since many recent studies have called into question the thesis that pre-monarchic Israel existed as an amphictyony.[8]

Specifically, it will be argued that the phrase "fear not" (אל תירא) occurs frequently in the Hebrew Scriptures in conjunction with other regularly recurring structural elements which make it possible to identify "fear not" as part of stereotypical language used to address a warrior to give comfort and assurance before an impending battle or an envisaged war. The study will also highlight important insights into the textual setting *(Sitz im Text)* of a passage when a "fear not" pericope is identified as manifesting the conventions of war.

It must be emphasized that, although the study uses form critical methodology, its aim is not to discern the origins of the form in an institutional setting *(Sitz im Leben)* but to explore the rhetorical features of the form as it is used in its present context. In this sense the study takes up the challenge of James Muilenburg in his well-known presidential address to the Society of Biblical Literature titled, "Form-Criticism and Beyond."[9] In many cases form criticism in its speculation about *Sitz im Leben* has anchored a form in a social institution, ignoring the literary setting in which a given representative of a form occurs. Such a procedure assumes that the form is static when, in fact, it is dynamically adapted to a variety of settings. In short, past studies have defined a form in terms of its birth rather than its life. Both Begrich and von Rad were concerned with the origins or settings of forms in the institutional life of Israel. Their speculation about origins ignored how a particular form functioned in its existing literary contexts. In their failure to be attentive to the present literary context of a form, they also ignored the clearest evidence of the form's identity.

The Organization of the Study

The study will begin in Chapter I with the Deuteronomic History because the prose narrative here makes it clear that "fear not" is used to comfort a warrior or warriors before a battle. Here the larger form containing the phrase "fear not" will be identified. It will be shown that the structure of the form will vary somewhat depending on the specific situation, e.g., whether the coming battle is an offensive battle or a defensive battle. A major element of the form in the Deuteronomic History is that a warrior is given Orders for the impending battle. When Yahweh speaks to a warrior, the warrior is expected to be an active participant in the conflict. It will be noted, however, that the genre is not used exclusively as a divine form of speech; it can be used by a human being to comfort a warrior.

Chapter II will treat "fear not" texts in Jeremiah where the form is utilized to comfort Jeremiah as a warrior prophet in much the same way as the form is used in the Deuteronomic History to comfort Elijah as a warrior prophet.

The use of the form by Isaiah in War Oracles addressed to king Ahaz and king Hezekiah will be the subject of Chapter III. In these royal settings the form is used in a somewhat different way than in the Deuteronomic History and in Jeremiah. The king is not ordered to be an active participant in war; he is to take a passive stance. He is either ordered not to fight or is promised that Yahweh will fight for him. Here there will be some discussion of the form in extra-biblical texts addressed to kings.

The fourth chapter will deal with the use of the form in association with building the temple as a citadel against the enemy in the Chronicler's History and in Haggai. Here it will be indicated that the role of the king is to offer praise to Yahweh who does the fighting.

"Fear not" texts in Second Isaiah will be the focus of Chapter V. These exilic texts comfort the community as king. Like a king, the community is not to be an active participant in the coming warfare. The active warfare of the community is over. Interestingly, the community's identity here is not linked with the pre-eminent warriors of the past, Moses and Joshua, but with the ancestor Abraham. Like the patriarchs, Jacob/Israel is promised "offspring" (זרע). Yahweh's promise to wage peace for Israel among the nations parallels Yahweh's promise to the ancient ancestors of Israel that they will be a blessing to the nations.

The sixth chapter will discuss other proto-apocalyptic texts that share characteristics of the form as it is used by Second Isaiah.

The study will conclude in Chapters VII and VIII with a discussion of the "fear not" form in Genesis and Exodus. In the patriarchal narratives the form is similar in function to the form in Second Isaiah. Yahweh promises the patriarchs "offspring" and wages peace for them when they encounter warfare. In Exodus, for example, the form is used to order the community, like a king, to be still while Yahweh achieves victory for Israel at the Sea.

Each chapter will contain a technical study of the language of the "fear not" pericopes under consideration as well as an examination of the larger contexts of the pericopes. This procedure permits the genre in the Hebrew Scriptures to be studied not in terms of its origins but in terms of the life it has had in the literary traditions of ancient Israel. No attempt is made to trace this life chronologically as if various uses of the form in the literary traditions can be ranked according to stages of development. The varied uses of the form can be explained not by historical change but by the purposes of the various authors who used it. The structure of the study is not meant to reflect the historical development of the form but the pattern of the form's use in the text of the Hebrew Scriptures as we now have it. That the study ends with Genesis and Exodus is not necessarily meant to suggest that this is the latest use of the form; rather, the use of the form to address the patriarchs reflects the pattern of the proto-apocalyptic texts in which the form is used to comfort the community as king.

Broadly speaking the form in the Hebrew Scriptures reflects two major uses. In the Deuteronomic History and in Jeremiah the form associated with "fear not" is used to order a warrior or warriors to participate actively in battle. In other appearances of the form in the Hebrew Scriptures, the king (or the community addressed as king) is ordered to take a passive stance in warfare; the deity promises that he alone will fight for the king. These two primary uses of the genre reflect two complexes of tradition which scholars have frequently identified in the Hebrew Scriptures: a Mosaic tradition stressing the responsible actions of the community for the maintenance of the covenant and a Davidic or royal tradition emphasizing the responsible actions of the deity for the maintenance of the covenant.

A Note on Terminology

In the study I have sometimes used the general terminology "language of war" or "language of address to a warrior" to refer to the genre associated with "fear not." This general terminology reflects the fact that in the Hebrew Scriptures the genre is used as a human as well as a divine form of speech. The term "War Oracle" refers to the genre only when the speaker is a deity.

CHAPTER I

"FEAR NOT" IN THE DEUTERONOMIC HISTORY

Introduction

Although the occurrence of the phrase "fear not" does not necessarily suggest a war setting, "fear not" occurs most frequently in the Deuteronomic History in contexts associated with the conduct of war. To begin a study of "fear not" pericopes in the Hebrew Scriptures with the Deuteronomic History is particularly appropriate because the prose narrative provides the clearest examples of the form in settings which make its function obvious. Warriors such as Moses and pre-eminently Joshua are comforted with "fear not" language before going into battle and are given orders concerning their active participation in battle.

Each of the "fear not" pericopes considered here will be examined closely to ascertain its structure: the elements it contains, its order, and its formulation. After scrutiny of the conventions of the language in the pericopes, the literary settings of the phrase "fear not" and its associated elements will be studied to determine the relationship between structure and context and the meaning of variations in structure of the language of war associated with "fear not." Thus we will discern that addresses to warriors in situations of defense differ in structure from addresses in situations of offense or when war is spoken of generally or abstractly, as when no particular battle is imminent. Study of the pericopes in the chapter will also indicate that "fear not" is not peculiar to the language Yahweh uses to address a warrior but is typical as well of language used when a human being addresses a warrior, so that links to a specific cultic institution such as holy or sacred war cannot be assumed.

Yahweh Addresses a Warrior: Deut 3:2 (//Num 21:34); Josh 8:1-2; 10:8 and 11:6

1.   *Structure*

Our analysis of "fear not" pericopes in the Deuteronomic History will begin with four texts in which Yahweh speaks directly to a warrior. Structurally, these texts are quite similar. With a few variations, each one begins with "fear not" (Assurance), indicates what the warrior should not fear (Object of Fear), explains why the warrior should not fear (Basis of Assurance) and tells the warrior what his role will be (Orders and/or

Directives). The pericopes are reproduced below with their elements labeled to permit comparison of structural similarities.

Deut 3:2 (//Num 21:34)

(a)   ASSURANCE

"Do not fear
אל תירא

(b)   OBJECT OF FEAR

him;
אתו

(c)   BASIS OF ASSURANCE

for I have given him and all his people and his land into your hand;
כי בידך נתתי אתו ואת כל עמו ואת ארצו

(d)   ORDERS

and you shall do to him as you did to Sihon the king of the Amorites, who dwelt at Heshbon."
ועשית לו כאשר עשית לסיחן מלך האמרי אשר יושב בחשבון

Josh 8:1-2

(a)   ASSURANCE

"Do not fear or be dismayed;
אל תירא ואל תחת

(b)   DIRECTIVE

take all the fighting men with you, and arise, go up to Ai;
קח עמך את כל עם המלחמה וקום עלה העי

(c)   BASIS OF ASSURANCE

see, I have given into your hand the king of Ai, and his people, his city, and his land;
ראה נתתי בידך את מלך העי ואת עמו ואת עירו ואת ארצו

(d)   ORDERS

and you shall do to Ai and its king as you did to Jericho and its king; only its spoil and its cattle you shall take as booty for yourselves;
ועשית לעי ולמלכה כאשר עשית ליריחו ולמלכה רק שללה ובהמתה ובזו לכם

(e)   DIRECTIVE

       lay an ambush against the city, behind it."
                                שים לך ארב לעיר מאחריה

Josh 10:8

(a)   ASSURANCE

       "Do not fear
                        אל ונירא

(b)   OBJECT OF FEAR

       them,
               מהם

(c)   BASIS OF ASSURANCE

       for I have given them into your hand;[1]
                                כי בידך נותים

(d)   ORDERS

       there shall not a man of them stand before you."
                                לא יעמד איש מהם בפניך

Josh 11:6

(a)   ASSURANCE

       "Do not be afraid
                        אל תירא

(b)   OBJECT OF FEAR

       of them,
                  מפניהם

(c)   BASIS OF ASSURANCE

       for tomorrow at this time, I will give over all of them, slain, to Israel;
                    כי מחר כעת הזאת אנכי נתן את כלם חללים לפני ישראל

(d)   ORDERS

       you shall hamstring their horses, and burn their chariots with fire."
                        את סוסיהם העקר ואון מרכבתיהם תשרף באש

Three of these texts are virtually the same in structure, and the fourth is closely related. Deut 3:2 (//Num 21:34); Josh 10:8 and 11:6 all have an Assurance, an Object of Fear, a Basis of Assurance and Orders; and these four elements of the structure appear in the same order. Furthermore, the elements are similarly formulated. The Assurance is the phrase, אל תירא. The Basis of Assurance is introduced by the particle כי, and Yahweh speaks in the first person singular. The common phrase used here is "I have given" (נתתי) someone "into your hand" (בידך).[2] The Orders in Deut 3:2 (//Num 21:34) and Josh 11:6 are formulated in the second person singular and contain either imperfect verbs or perfect *waw* consecutives. The Orders in Josh 10:8 contain a verb in the third person rather than the expected second person. However, Joshua is referred to in the second person (בפניך), and the phrase which states that no one will stand before Joshua implies his active role in the battle: that he has orders to obey.

Josh 8:1-2 is somewhat distinctive. While it has an Assurance and Orders, like the other three texts, it does not contain an Object of Fear, and the Basis of Assurance is introduced by the imperative, ראה, rather than the particle כי. Also, it contains a Directive (an element that occurs twice). These apparent anomalies in Josh 8:1-2 can be clarified, however, by considering the way these words of address to a warrior function in their textual setting.

Despite the structural variation in Josh 8:1-2, the purpose of all these words of address to a warrior is to offer comfort and reassurance before battle. The Assurance and the Basis of Assurance stating that Yahweh has placed the enemies at Israel's disposal, serve to alleviate the warrior's fear of an impending battle and to support the carrying out of Orders given to the warrior for the ensuing military engagement. One should neither fear nor hesitate to carry out orders to participate in the battle because the results of the battle are announced beforehand; Yahweh has given the enemies into the hand of the warrior. All of these pericopes have the same purpose; but what is the significance of the structural variation between Josh 8:1-2 and the other three texts? The textual settings suggest that three of the four pericopes—Deut 3:2 (//Num 21:34); Josh 10:8 and Josh 11:6—are spoken in defensive situations and that Josh 8:1-2 is spoken in an offensive situation. In a defensive situation, the words of address to a warrior refer to the attacking enemies by employing the structural element we have called the Object of Fear. In an offensive situation, the words of address to a warrior refer to the call to initiate a battle by employing the structural element we have called the Directive.

A more detailed discussion of the literary contexts of these pericopes will illustrate the difference between the words of address to a warrior in a defensive situation and those in an offensive situation. Also, a discussion of the literary contexts will indicate that the words are not only intended to alleviate fear but to give orders for the impending battle to the warrior from his superior.

2.   *Textual Setting*

The context of Deut 3:2 (//Num 21:34) indicates that the words are spoken to the warrior Moses in a defensive situation and that he is given orders by his superior, Yahweh, for the coming defensive battle. The passage begins by indicating that Og the king of Bashan is the aggressor; all his people came out "to do battle (למלחמה) at Edrei" (Deut 3:1; Num 21:34). In Yahweh's address to his warrior Moses in this defensive situation, he refers to the attacking enemy—the Object of Fear—when he says, "Do not fear him" (אל תירא אתו). The Orders given to Moses—to do to Og, king of Bashan, as was done to Sihon, king of the Amorites—are promptly carried out.

In Deut 3:3 (see Num 21:35) it is reported by Moses,

> So the LORD our God gave into our hand Og also, king of Bashan, and all his people; and we smote him until no survivor was left to him.

Deut 3:6 makes it clear that the specific orders were carried out to the letter.

> And we utterly destroyed them, as we did to Sihon the king of Heshbon, destroying every city, men, women and children.

The words Yahweh speaks to Joshua in Josh 10:8 function similarly to those in Deut 3:2 (//Num 21:34); in both places the situation is a defensive one. In the Josh 10 passage we are told that enemies had come to make war against Gibeon, and they are mentioned by name:

> Then the five kings of the Amorites, the king of Jerusalem, the king of Hebron, the king of Jarmuth, the king of Lachish, and the king of Eglon gathered their forces, and went up with their armies and encamped against Gibeon and made war against it (וילחמו עליה).
>
> —Josh 10:5

According to the passage Joshua complies with the request of the Gibeonites to aid in their defense at Gilgal. In this defensive situation, Yahweh refers to the attacking enemies when he addresses his warrior Joshua, saying, "Do not fear them." The ensuing context makes it clear that the Orders given to Joshua, "there shall not a man of them stand before you," are carried out. In vs. 20 we are told that when Joshua and the sons of Israel "finished slaying them with a great slaughter" (ככלות...להכותם מכה גדולה מאד), "they were wiped out" (המם), and only a remnant of them remained to retreat to their fortified cities. However, Joshua continues his relentless pursuit. He traps the kings in a cave and later executes them. Chapter 10 ends with an account of lightning attacks throughout southern Palestine. Joshua follows his orders not to let a man stand before him. When he took Makkedah "he utterly destroyed every person in it, he left none remaining" (10:28). Similar massacres occurred in city after city (Libnah, Lachish, Gezer, Eglon, Hebron, Debir) until Joshua's orders were carried out,

> So Joshua defeated the whole land, the hill country and the Negeb
> and the lowland and the slope, and all their kings *he left none*
> *remaining, but utterly destroyed all that breathed, as the LORD God*
> *of Israel commanded.*
>
> —Josh 10:40

Josh 11:6, manifesting the same structure as Deut 3:2 (//Num 21:34) and Josh 10:8, functions similarly in a context of defensive war. Verses 1-4 mention the enemies by name and indicate that the kings had formed a coalition to fight against Israel.

> And all these kings joined their forces, and came and encamped
> together at the waters of Meron, to fight with Israel.
>
> —Josh 11:5

It is in this context that Yahweh speaks to Joshua who is engaged in a defensive battle and assures him that he need not fear these enemies, "Do not be afraid of them" (אל תירא מפניהם). Yahweh also gives Joshua specific orders, "you shall hamstring their horses and burn their chariots with fire." Again the subsequent narrative makes it clear that Joshua complied with the orders of Yahweh in the battle,

> And Joshua did to them as the LORD bade him; he hamstrung their
> horses, and burned their chariots with fire.
>
> —Josh 11:9

The three texts that are most clearly related in structure (Deut 3:2 [//Num 21:34]; Josh 10:8 and Josh 11:6), i.e., those texts which contain an Object of Fear, are also clearly related in setting. They are addressed to warriors in defensive situations.

Josh 8:1-2 is unique among the four texts in that it lacks an Object of Fear and has Directives. The first Directive, which takes the place of the Object of Fear in the structure, is a general command to engage in the battle; the second Directive clarifies specifically what has to be done. The textual setting of Yahweh's address to his warrior Joshua makes it clear that the fear is not occasioned by the necessity for Israel to defend herself against an enemy who has come to battle as in Deut 3:2 (//Num 21:34), Josh 10:8 and Josh 11:6. In Josh 8, the fear is occasioned by the command of Yahweh to attack. Yahweh is placing Israel on the offensive. The Directive to engage in battle takes the place of the Object of Fear; the variation in the structure reflects a different situation. Instead of enemies who are the Object of Fear, the Directive of Yahweh to engage in an offensive battle is the cause of fear.

The ensuing context indicates that Joshua acts to carry out strictly the Directives and Orders of Yahweh. In 8:3 we are told, "So Joshua arose, and all the fighting men, to go up to Ai." This is a response to the initial Directive of Yahweh to initiate battle; "take all the fighting men with you, and arise, go up to Ai." In vs. 4ff. we are told of the plans for the ambush and its successful completion. This fulfills the second Directive to "lay ambush against the city, behind it." Verse 27 shows that Joshua acts to carry out the specific Orders given.

> Only the cattle and the spoil of that city Israel took as their booty,
> according to the word of the LORD which he commanded Joshua.

In Josh 8, then, Yahweh's words, "Do not fear or be dismayed," to the warrior Joshua function to give assurance before battle. Joshua is not to be afraid of carrying out specific orders to engage in a battle of offense. The peculiar structure of these words of Yahweh to a warrior—the missing Object of Fear and the unique Directives—is explained by the offensive nature of the campaign.

To summarize the discussion thus far, we can say that these four "fear not" texts in the Deuteronomic History in which Yahweh speaks to a warrior have a typical structure and function. The peculiarity of the structure of Josh 8:1-2 can be explained by the different but related function it performs, i.e., it is addressed to Joshua in an offensive rather than a defensive situation.

The addresses to warriors in both defensive and offensive situations have a similar function, however, as is clear from their textual settings. They serve to assure the leader of the troops that there is no need to fear because Yahweh has already acted to deliver the enemy into Israel's hand, and they give Yahweh's specific orders for the leader and his troops to follow in the battle.

The analysis of these four "fear not" passages in the Deuteronomic History reflects the fact that we are dealing with conventional and stereotypical language used to address warriors before a battle. In order to determine whether this convention is to be attributed to the Deuteronomic Historian or whether it is a more nearly universal convention, we will need to examine other "fear not" pericopes in the Deuteronomic History in this chapter and to study "fear not" pericopes in other Old Testament and extra-biblical passages in subsequent chapters.

Moses on the Offensive: Deut 1:20-21

These are not words of address from Yahweh to a warrior. Rather Moses is recalling orders which Yahweh had given to all Israel for the offensive onslaught into the land of the Amorites. The importance of this pericope for our discussion is that the speech of Moses, recalling what Yahweh had ordered the people to do in this offensive military situation, uses structural elements very much like those in the address of Yahweh to the warrior Joshua in Josh 8:1-2 where Joshua was ordered to engage in an offensive military battle. This pericope thus lends support to the thesis that in situations of military offense the language of address to a warrior is structured in a stereotypical way.

The words of Moses in Deut 1:20-21 can be outlined as follows:

(a)   INTRODUCTION

>   You have come to the hill country of the Amorites, which the LORD our God gives us.
>
>   באתם עד הר האמרי אשר יהוה אלהינו נתן לנו

(b)   BASIS OF ASSURANCE

>   Behold, the LORD your God has set the land before you;
>
>   ראה נתן יהוה אלהיך לפניך את הארץ

(c)   DIRECTIVE

>   go up, take possession,
>
>   עלה רש

(d)   REFERENCE TO ORDERS

>   as the LORD, the God of your fathers, has told you;
>
>   כאשר דבר יהוה אלהי אבתיך לך

   (e)   ASSURANCE

> do not fear or be dismayed.
>
> אל תירא ואל תחת

The similarities to Josh 8:1-2 are as follows: (a) The Assurance "do not fear or be dismayed" (אל תירא ואל וחת) is exactly the same. (b) In both places the Basis of Assurance is introduced by the imperative ראה and not the particle כי; typically the verb נתן is used. (c) There is a Directive, not an Object of Fear. The exhortation not to fear concerns the fear of initiating an offensive battle, as in Josh 8:1-2, rather than the fear of enemies who threaten to attack. (d) There are no specific Orders given here as in Josh 8:1-2, but there is a reference to the orders Yahweh had given to the people.

This pericope, then, is another example showing that in offensive situations the language of address to a warrior employing the phrase "fear not" has a peculiar formulation. There is a Directive rather than an Object of Fear; the Basis of Assurance is introduced by ראה rather than כי; and the Assurance is longer than the simple אל תירא.

General Regulations for Waging War: Deut 20:3-4

This text occurs in the legal corpus of Deuteronomy and concerns the words a priest is to speak to the community before battle.[3] Unlike the texts we have discussed thus far, Deut 20:3-4 is concerned not with a particular battle but with the regulations for the general conduct of war.

> And when you draw near to the battle, the priest shall come forward
> and speak to the people.
>
> —Deut 20:2

Since the situation concerns the general conduct of war rather than a specific battle, it should not be surprising that the structure of the priest's words, while having affinities with both offensive and defensive war language, is another variation of the conventional language of war considered thus far. A discussion of the structure of this pericope will point out both similarities to and differences from the texts previously discussed and identify the reasons for the variations in structure. The structure of the priest's words is as follows:

(a)   SUMMONS TO HEAR

Hear,
שמע

(b)   ADDRESS

O Israel, you draw near this day to battle against your enemies:
ישראל אתם קרבים היום למלחמה על איביכם

(c)   ASSURANCE

let not your heart faint; do not fear, or tremble, or be in dread
אל ירך לבבכם אל תיראו ואל תחפזו ואל תערצו

(d)   OBJECT OF FEAR

of them;
מפניהם

(e)   BASIS OF ASSURANCE

for the LORD your God is he that goes with you,
כי יהוה אלהיכם ההלך עמכם

(f)   PROMISE

to fight for you against your enemies, to give you the victory.
להלחם לכם עם איביכם להושיע אתכם

Like the others considered thus far, this text has an Assurance, an Object of Fear
and a Basis of Assurance. However, except in the case of the Object of Fear, these
elements are formulated somewhat differently. While we noted above that in Josh 8:1-2
the Assurance is expanded with the parallel phrase ואל תחת, the Assurance here is
expanded by three additional phrases. Here also it should be noted that the verbs are in
the plural rather than the singular and are addressed to the community rather than an
individual warrior. The Basis of Assurance is introduced by the particle כי as in the
defensive war language, but it does not contain the phrase, "I (Yahweh) have given (נתן)
someone into your hand (בידך)." It rather refers to Yahweh in the third person and
describes him as "your God who goes with you" (אלהיכם ההלך עמכם).

Furthermore, this text contains structural elements that are not present in the other
texts we have discussed. These three additional elements are:

(1)   A Summons to Hear.

(2)   An Address. Notice the use of the pronoun אתם, a point that will be significant

in later discussions.

(3)   A Promise. This is not an Order which concerns what Israel is to do but a
      promise of what Yahweh will do for "you" (Israel).   Notice the infinitive
      construction; this point will be significant in later discussion.

The variations in the structure of this text, however, are understandable in view of the
reason for the speech. Just as the conventional language of war will vary depending on
whether it is given before an offensive or defensive engagement, so the structure of the
language will vary depending on whether it concerns the general conduct of war or a
specific war situation.   Another difference between this text and those previously
discussed should be mentioned. The others were addressed to a war leader; this oracle is
addressed to the community.[4] The purpose of this priestly oracle is to give orders not to
a military leader but to the community being exhorted to fight. In such a situation the
Summons to Hear and the Address which states the reason for the speech ("you draw near
this day to battle against your enemies") are appropriate. The expanded Assurance is
characteristic of exhortation, as can also be seen in the offensive war speech in Josh
8:1-2 which, though commanding that a battle be initiated, has a tone of exhortation and
expands the Assurance. In Deut 20:3-4 there are no specific orders because no specific
battle is envisaged. The general Promise for those who fight for Yahweh is given; when
one fights for Yahweh, Yahweh will also fight against the enemy and give "you" the
victory. The context makes it clear that, when a specific battle does occur, Israel as
warrior will have specific orders to obey. The Address says, "you draw near this day *to*
fight (למלחמה) against your enemies."   The regulations which follow clarify the
preparations the warriors should make before they fight.

So far, then, we have seen in the Deuteronomic History conventional formulations
which vary somewhat depending on the specific occasion on which they are used. There
are addresses to warriors which are spoken to leaders in a defensive campaign; these vary
somewhat from those spoken to leaders in an offensive campaign. Both types specify the
particular orders to be carried out. The oracle described in Deut 20:3-4 is addressed to
the community and does not give the specific orders to be carried out in a particular
military campaign by a leader in the battle. It concerns the conduct of war generally and
describes Yahweh's overall action in the midst of the people as a warrior.

The picture that is beginning to emerge in our study of "fear not" pericopes in war contexts is that, on the one hand, it is possible to speak about a conventional formulation of the language of address to a warrior functioning typically as words of encouragement before engagement in battle. On the other hand, the structure of the language will vary somewhat depending on the specific situation in which it is used. It is too general to speak simply of a war setting. It is more proper and precise to speak about various settings in war and the corresponding variations in the form or structure of conventional language used to address a warrior. In short, the specific war setting gives rise to a particular formulation of the genre. There are many elements typical of the language of address to a warrior, not the least of which is the formula "fear not." But not all the elements always occur in a specific example of the genre because the particular setting will demand a particular formulation of the language requiring some elements in its structure and not others. For example, the structure will vary depending on who is addressed (a leader or the community) or on the situation (a defensive battle or an offensive battle, a specific battle or a more general situation).

The Conventional Language of War Spoken by a Human Warrior

Up to this point we have been considering texts where Yahweh, the divine warrior, or his representative speaks to a warrior or warriors. What we hope to show now is that the conventional formulation of address to a warrior is not peculiar to divine speech but is characteristic also of the language of war spoken by human beings. When Yahweh speaks as a warrior to other warriors, the same conventional elements of war language are used as when one human warrior addresses another. The structural form of Yahweh's words addressed either to Israel or its leaders does not point to a particular institution of holy war but is associated with the conventions of language associated with the practice of war generally.

1.   2 Sam 13:28

These words of Absalom appear in an account of plans for the assassination of Amnon to incite revolt in the Davidic kingdom. Notice that the words are spoken by Absalom to his servants, "Then Absalom commanded his servants" (vs. 28). They concern an "offensive" military act initiating internal warfare in David's house. The words are outlined as follows:

(a)   DIRECTIVE

Mark when Amnon's heart is merry with wine and when I say to you, "Strike Amnon,"

ראו נא כטוב לב אמנון ביין ואמרתי אליכם הכו את אמנון

(b)   ORDERS

then you will kill him.[5]

והמתם אתו

(c)   ASSURANCE

Fear not;

אל תיראו

(d)   BASIS OF ASSURANCE

have I not commanded you?

הלוא כי אנכי צויתי אתכם

(e)   ENCOURAGEMENT

Be courageous and be valiant.

חזקו והיו לבני חיל

Since these words are addressed to rebels who are to commit an offensive act, it should not be surprising that they are formulated similarly to the offensive language of address to warriors we have looked at thus far. The elements of the conventional language of war here and in Josh 8:1-2 are nearly the same. The elements are: Directive, Orders, Assurance, Basis of Assurance and Encouragement (Josh 8:1-2 had a concluding Directive), the only difference being that the elements are in somewhat different order. The Directive is in the imperative, the Orders are given in the second person, and the Assurance is the expected אל תיראו.   The peculiarities of the formulation of the language reflect the particular war setting in which they occur.   In the texts we considered earlier in which Yahweh was the speaker, the Basis of Assurance grounded the Assurance not to fear on the fact that Yahweh had given the enemy into the hand of the warrior. The Basis of Assurance is a rhetorical question in 2 Sam 13:28 and assures those who carry out the assassination plot that they need not fear. Who can question the royal command to carry out the assassination? The Encouragement in 2 Sam 13:28 employs vocabulary which is also typical of war. חזק is frequently used in the imperative to encourage person(s) in a military setting to fulfill a military task to which they have just been appointed. (For a fuller discussion see below pp. 25-27 ff.) Here Absalom encourages the assassins to get on with their difficult task. Notice how the textual setting of this pericope indicates that the orders were carried out, "So the servants of Absalom did to Amnon as Absalom had commanded" (vs. 29a).

2.   *2 Kgs 25:24//Jer 40:9-10*

This pericope provides us with yet another military situation. Here we have the address of a governor, Gedaliah, to the military forces (2 Kgs 25:23; Jer 40:7-8) concerning their role under the rule of the Babylonians. The situation is one in which Gedaliah calls for peaceful co-existence with the new ruling military regime. The oracle can be outlined as follows:

(a)   ASSURANCE

>   Do not be afraid
>   אל תיראו

(b)   OBJECT OF FEAR

>   because of the Chaldean officials;
>   מעבדי הכשדים

(c)   DIRECTIVE

>   dwell in the land, and serve the king of Babylon,
>   שבו בארץ ועבדו את מלך בבל

(d)   BASIS OF ASSURANCE

>   and it shall be well with you.
>   וייטב לכם

(e)   ORDERS[6]

>   As for me, I will dwell at Mizpah, to stand for you before the Chaldeans who will come to us; but as for you, gather wine and summer fruits and oil, and store them in your vessels, and dwell in your cities that you have taken.
>   ואני הנני ישב במצפה לעמד לפני הכשדים אשר יבאו אלינו ואתם אספו יין
>   וקיץ ושמן ושמו בכליכם ושבו בעריכם אשר תפשתם

The following points will clarify how the specific situation affects the actual formulation of the language of war:

(1)   Since the situation is one of military domination by another power and is therefore a defensive situation, one could expect an Object of Fear. This element does indeed occur and is formulated typically with

(2)   Yet these words also contain a Directive. We have been arguing that the
Directive is typical of offensive and not defensive situations. However, the defensive
situation here is unusual. This language is not used as a prelude to a defensive battle
because a defensive battle is not feasible for a military force that has already been
overpowered. Therefore, a Directive is given not to attack but to dwell peacefully in the
land. Ironically, the situation of defense here calls for a kind of offense—to initiate a
life of peaceful co-existence with the enemy, and this fact is reflected in the use of a
Directive.

(3)   The Basis of Assurance, like that in 2 Sam 13:28, is formulated somewhat
freely.

(4)   The Orders (found only in the expanded text of Jeremiah), like the Directive,
concern peaceful co-existence and not the specific orders for a coming battle. Here the
Orders are formulated with imperatives—not commonly the case. Imperatives mostly
characterize the Directive. These two elements, the Directive and the Orders, are very
closely related, and in the concluding part of this section we will more clearly define the
similarites and differences between them.

These words of Gedaliah, then, indicate that the language of address to a warrior
can be extended in usage to situations where no actual battle is envisaged. The warriors
Gedaliah addresses are a defeated army. The situation is not an offensive or defensive
battle nor is the general prospect of war a concern. Therefore, the structure of
Gedaliah's words is not designed to comfort a warrior before a battle but to comfort a
defeated army living under the rule of a conquering enemy. The enemy still exists as a
threat so the Object of Fear, characteristic of addresses in defensive situations, is used.
However, the new situation of being a conquered army requires new initiatives, and
therefore, a Directive, characteristic of addresses in offensive situations, is employed.
The Directive, however, is not to initiate a battle but to initiate a new style for defeated
warriors.

That the address to a warrior can sometimes be used in situations where military
action is only marginal to the situation is evident from two other passages which need to
be discussed, namely Jonathan's address to David (1 Sam 23:17) and David's address to
Mephibosheth (2 Sam 9:7). In neither situation is a warrior comforted before a military
campaign. However, the language of address to a warrior is extended to these two

situations where the one addressed has experienced the ravages of war.

3.   *l Sam 23:17*

This passage concerns a situation in which Saul sought to kill David because David was a threat to his kingship. The setting is thus the military intrigue associated with the challenge to leadership. The passage says that David "was afraid" (וירא, vs. 15) when he discovered Saul's intentions. Jonathan comes to David and comforts him with words which can be outlined as follows:

(a)   ASSURANCE

    Fear not;
    אל תירא

(b)   BASIS OF ASSURANCE

    for the hand of Saul my father shall not find you;
    כי לא ומצאך יד שאול אבי

(c)   ORDERS (?)

    you shall be king over Israel, and I shall be next to you; Saul my father also knows this.
    ואתה תמלך על ישראל ואנכי אהיה לך למשנה וגם שאול אבי ידע כן

These words of Jonathan clarify the specific military situation. It is one which concerns the transfer of power, and Jonathan is informing David that he will not challenge David's rise to power even though he has a rightful claim to the throne. These words of Jonathan are typical of the conventional language of war. There are the typical Assurance and the Basis of Assurance. Notice here that the Basis of Assurance is introduced by the particle כי. The rest of the phrase used in the Basis of Assurance is also reminiscent of other texts we have considered. In texts where Yahweh speaks, Yahweh assures the recipient of an address that he has given an enemy "into your hand" (בידך). Here Jonathan assures David that the "hand" (יד) of Saul will not find him. Jonathan assures David that he will not give him into Saul's hand. There is no Object of Fear as might be expected in war language where the one addressed is in a defensive situation. However, Saul, the object of David's fear, is mentioned in the Basis of Assurance. One element of Jonathan's words parallels what we have been calling the Orders. We have marked this element with a question mark in our outline of the structure of this text for, even though the Orders are typically formulated in the second person, the "Orders" are really a concession by Jonathan that David will be king. This

anomaly is explained by the fact that the speaker here is an inferior and not a superior

party. It should be pointed out that the concession or relinquishing of power by Jonathan

leads to the making of a covenant or treaty between David and Jonathan, "And the two

of them made a covenant before the LORD . . ." (23:18a)   David's acceptance of

Jonathan's concession ended in a truce.

4.   2 Sam 9:7

This text occurs in a situation where David offers protection or asylum to

Mephibosheth, a member of the defeated house of Saul, the enemy. When Mephibosheth

is brought into David's presence, David says,

   (a)   ASSURANCE

         Do not fear;
         אל תירא

   (b)   BASIS OF ASSURANCE

         for I will show you kindness for the sake of your father Jonathan, and I will
         restore to you all the land of Saul your father;
         כי עשה אעשה עמך חסד בעבור יהונתן אביך והשבתי לך את כל שדה שאול אביך

   (c)   ORDERS

         and you shall eat at my table always.
         ואתה תאכל לחם על שלחני תמיד

Here there are three typical elements characteristic of the conventional war speech

addressed to an individual in a defensive situation: the Assurance, the Basis of Assurance

typically introduced by the particle כי and formulated in the first person singular, and

the Orders typically formulated in the second person. There is not an Object of Fear

because the object of fear, David, speaks the words himself.

It will be helpful at this point to summarize our findings thus far. We have argued

that in the Deuteronomic History there was a conventional way of constructing the

language of Yahweh when he addressed warriors. This conventional language was

identified on the basis of typically recurring structural elements used in conjunction with

"fear not." The formation and use of the elements was determined by the specific

situation of war. We have now noted that this conventional language is not unique to the

construction of divine speech but is also typical of the language of war used when one human warrior addresses another warrior. Our discussion of the secular language of war has illustrated how the specific use of the conventional language of war will affect the construction of a particular address. Assassination plots, the call for peaceful co-existence, the relinquishing of the throne, the offer of asylum—all occasion the use of the conventional language of war; the convention, however, is affected by the setting.

Preparations for Conquest: Deut 31:1-8

These are words of Moses addressed to the people of Israel and to Joshua as leader. They concern the passing on of leadership to Joshua before the conquest of the land—a conquest in which Moses is not able to participate. Moses exhorts Israel and Joshua to discharge faithfully their respective responsibilities before entering the land to take possession of it. As might be expected, this passage employs conventional language of war.

On the one hand Moses states that Yahweh will be the warrior who will fight for Israel. He says, "The LORD your God will go over before you" (יהוה אלהיך הוא עבר לפניך) and "he will destroy these nations before you" (הוא ישמיד את הגוים האלה מלפניך). He adds further, "And the LORD will do to them as he did to Sihon and Og, the kings of the Amorites, and to their land, when he destroyed them" (vss. 3-4). Yet, on the other hand, it is clear that Israel will be involved in the battle and will be given orders for the conquest that is envisaged. Israel will not sit passively while Yahweh fights the battle. Moses tells the people, "you shall dispossess them" (וירשתם) and adds, "Joshua will go over (עבר) at your head, as the LORD has spoken." In vss. 5-6 Moses addresses the people as warriors, giving them their marching orders, and in vss. 7-8 he addresses Joshua as military leader. It will be helpful now to outline the structure of the language used by Moses:

(1)   To the people (vss. 5-6)

    (a)   BASIS OF ASSURANCE

        And the LORD will give them over to you,
        ונתנם יהוה לפניכם

(b)   ORDERS

and you shall do to them according to all the commandments which I
have commanded you.

ועשיתם להם ככל המצוה אשר צויתי אתכם

(c)   ENCOURAGEMENT

Be strong and of good courage,

חזקו ואמצו

(d)   ASSURANCE

do not fear or be in dread

אל תיראו ואל תערצו

(e)   OBJECT OF FEAR

of them:

מפניהם

(f)   BASIS OF ASSURANCE

for it is the LORD your God who goes with you;

כי יהוה אלהיך הוא ההלך עמך

(g)   PROMISE

he will not fail you or forsake you.

לא ירפך ולא יעזבך

(2)   To Joshua (vss. 7-8)

(a)   ENCOURAGEMENT

Be strong and of good courage;

חזק ואמץ

(b)   ORDERS

for you shall go with this people into the land which the LORD has sworn
to their fathers to give them; and you shall put them in possession of it.

כי אתה תבוא את העם הזה אל הארץ אשר נשבע יהוה לאבתם לתת להם ואתה
תנחילנה אותם

(c)   BASIS OF ASSURANCE

It is the LORD who goes before you; he will be with you;

ויהוה הוא ההלך לפניך הוא יהיה עמך

(d)   PROMISE

> he will not fail you or forsake you;
> לא ירפך ולא יעזבך

(e)   ASSURANCE

> do not fear or be dismayed.
> לא תירא ולא תחת

The first thing that should be pointed out about the structure of Moses' words to both Joshua and to the people is that, although they resemble those texts which address the general prospect of war (cf. Deut 20:3-4), they also employ formulaic elements characteristic of the language used before a specific battle. Moses has in view the general prospect of the conquest and therefore announces the promise that Yahweh will fight for Israel and Joshua; he also has the specific responsibilities of Joshua and the people in mind and thus gives them orders to follow. Notice that the Orders are stated quite generally as might be expected here and are not like the specific Orders given when a particular battle is to be fought. There is a Basis of Assurance in each address, stating that Yahweh your God goes with you. This is formulated very much as is the Basis of Assurance in Deut 20:3-4: a text which outlines in general what the priest is to say about military engagement. The Promise is exactly the same in both the address to the people and the address to Joshua; it states what will be the general prospect in the envisaged conquest. The words addressed to the people begin with a Basis of Assurance which is closely related to the recurring phrase (נתתי...בידך) in the texts in which Yahweh speaks to a warrior.

In short, then, the formulaic elements in these two addresses are typical of conventional language of war we have already considered. However, it will be necessary to discuss in greater detail the imperative phrase, חזק ואמץ, a phrase which occurs both in the address to Joshua and in the address to the people. (In the latter case it is of course in the plural.) Subsequent discussion will show that outside the Deuteronomic corpus, the imperative חזק, either used alone or in conjunction with אמץ, is typical of the conventional language of war. It is often connected with אל תירא, and most frequently, although not exclusively, occurs in texts which speak of the appointment of the warrior to a new task to be performed in his vocation as a warrior. The phrase חזק ואמץ is used with these connotations in, e.g., 1 Chr 22:13; 28:20; and 2 Chr 32:7; חזק is used alone in this sense in, e.g., Hag 2:4; 2 Chr 15:7 and 19:11.[7]

It is possible, however, to explain these connotations of the imperative חזק and the imperative phrase, חזק ואמץ, on the basis of their use in the Deuteronomic History. The first thing that should be said is that חזק and חזק ואמץ are not associated peculiarly with holy war as some have argued.[8] They are used also in language associated with the secular or mundane practice of war. It occurs in, e.g., the language Joab uses to address his brother, Abishai, as a warrior during one of David's wars. 2 Sam 10 records an incident of hostility between David and the Ammonites. In the conflict the Ammonites bought the services of the Syrians to help them in their war with David. In the course of the battle, Joab, David's military commander, found that he and his troops were penned between the Ammonites and the Syrians. The following words addressed to Joab's brother in 2 Sam 10:9-12 are Joab's battle tactics in face of this predicament; they are designed to encourage his brother in a new responsibility he has been given as warrior.

> When Joab saw that the battle was set against him both in front and
> in the rear, he chose some of the picked men of Israel, and arranged
> them against the Syrians; the rest of his men he put in the charge of
> Abishai his brother, and he arrayed them against the Ammonites.
> And he said, "If the Syrians are too strong (ותחזק) for me, then you
> will help me, but if the Ammonites are too strong (יחזקו) for you,
> then I will come and help you. Be of good courage (חזק) and let us
> take courage (ונתחזק)[10] for our people, and for the cities of our God;
> and may the LORD do what seems good to him.

                                              —2 Sam 10:9-13

The important thing to note about the use of the imperative חזק is that it is used as a word of encouragement addressed to Abishai and concerns the new task he has been given in his vocation as a warrior. He is to be strong in his mission as the newly appointed leader of the forces to fight the Ammonites.

חזק is similarly used by Absalom in his concluding Assurance to the servants he chose to assassinate Amnon in 2 Sam 13:28—a text we considered above. Absalom says to the servants who were given their new responsibility, "Be courageous and be valiant" (חזקו והיו לבני חיל). The imperative חזק used both in the words of Joab and in the words of Absalom are associated with the appointment of a warrior or warriors to a particular task to be performed in the conduct of war. They encourage the warrior(s) in his vocation as a warrior.

The phrase חזקו ואמצו is used in Josh 10:25—a text we also considered earlier in our discussion of the war oracle in Josh 10:8. Joshua speaks these words to the chiefs of the men of war in a ritual associated with the execution of the five captive kings that Joshua had just defeated. He tells the chiefs of the men of war to put their feet on the necks of the defeated kings and says to them,

> Do not be afraid or dismayed; be strong and of good courage (אל תיראו ואל תחתו חזקו ואמצו); for thus the LORD will do to all your enemies against whom you fight.

> —Josh 10:25

The words of Assurance (אל תיראו ואל תחתו) coupled with the words of Encouragement (חזקו ואמצו) are used as part of a ceremony which concerns the vocation of the chiefs of the men as warriors. They are being encouraged in their vocation as warriors.

The use of the phrase (חזק ואמץ) in the two texts we have been considering in Deut 31 is consistent with encouragement of a warrior in his new vocation. Moses is addressing the people as warriors and Joshua as a military leader in the new task that they have been given, i.e., to conquer the inhabitants of the land that had been promised to their fathers. The use of חזק ואמץ in this chapter is thus appropriate.

Indeed, the phrase חזק ואמץ is used once more in Deut 31 in vs. 23, and four times in Josh 1 (vss. 6, 7, 9 and 18). All of these instances concern the appointment of Joshua as the military leader of the people.

In this discussion of חזק ואמץ in Deut 31, the point that we have emphasized is that while this passage employs the conventional language of war as described earlier, the use of חזק ואמץ introduces a new motif into our discussion, i.e., a typical formulation of conventional language of war which functions to encourage the warrior when he is assigned a new and responsible war-related task to perform.

Isaiah's Prophetic War Oracle: 2 Kgs 19:6//Isa 37:6

We have still to address the question as to whether this stereotypical language used to address a warrior is purely a convention of the Deuteronomic "authors" or whether the convention spreads more broadly across Israelite literary traditions. Our argument that the convention is indeed larger than the Deuteronomic History will need to await an examination of "fear not" texts outside the Deuteronomic History. There is one text in

the Deuteronomic History, however, that indicates that the conventional use of war
language extends beyond the Deuteronomic literary tradition. A prophetic oracle of
Isaiah found in 2 Kgs 19:6 (paralleled in Isa 37:6) is suggestive of the pervasiveness of this
language in Israelite literary traditions.

These words spoken by the prophet Isaiah are delivered also in a situation of war.
The historical incident that provides the context for Isaiah's words is Sennacherib's
invasion of Judah and his siege of Jerusalem during the reign of Hezekiah. The specific
occasion is Hezekiah's consultation of Isaiah after the Rabshakeh's inflammatory and
threatening words in Jerusalem. Isaiah's prophetic oracle is spoken to the servants of
Hezekiah who are to relay the message to the king. The words can be outlined as
follows:

(a)   PROPHETIC MESSENGER FORMULA

Say to your master, "Thus says the LORD:
כה תאמרון אל אדניכם כה אמר יהוה

(b)   ASSURANCE

Do not be afraid
אל תירא

(c)   OBJECT OF FEAR

because of the words that you have heard, with which the servants of the king
of Assyria have reviled me.
מפני הדברים אשר שמעת אשר גדפו נערי מלך אשור אתי

(d)   BASIS OF ASSURANCE

Behold, I will put a spirit in him, so that he shall hear a rumor and return to
his own land;
הנני נתן בו רוח ושמע שמועה ושב לארצו

(e)   PROMISE

and I will cause him to fall by the sword in his own land."
והפלתיו בחרב בארצו

The structure of this address, which contains an Object of Fear, indicates that it is
spoken in a defensive situation. The distinctive elements in this structure can be
explained by the specific situation:

(1)   The Prophetic Messenger Formula occurs because this is a prophetic oracle,
and this formula is typical of prophetic speech.

(2)   The Object of Fear refers specifically to the words of the Rabshakeh because these words were the immediate expression of threat in this situation of war.

(3)   The Basis of Assurance is a variation of the typical formula that Yahweh had given the enemy into the hand of the warrior. Here Yahweh says in the first person, "Behold, I will put (נתן) a spirit in him. . ." The use of נתן and the first person singular formulation are typical of this element. Here the text does not say "I have given the enemy to you" because the emphasis is on Yahweh's handling of the affairs of war without human participation. Yahweh does not tell a warrior that he had placed the enemy at the warrior's disposal but that the enemy is placed at Yahweh's disposal. This brings us to our last observation about the specific formulation of this oracle.

(4)   There are no specific Orders as in the earlier addresses to warriors in defensive situations. As in Deut 20:3-4 which contained a Promise to the community, there is a Promise in 2 Kgs 19:6. This highlights an important observation: the unique input of the individual in using typical forms of speech. It has been long observed that Isaiah of Jerusalem employs the Zion theology, which places sole emphasis on Yahweh as a warrior and attributes to the king and the community a more passive stance of faith.[9] This theological tradition is reflected in 2 Kgs 19:6. The king does not receive orders to fight in a battle; instead Yahweh will protect Jerusalem by defeating the Assyrian king in his own way and without human participation. Perhaps this oracle preserves "authentic" words of Isaiah. At any rate the structure of this prophetic address to Hezekiah is closely related to Isaiah's more famous prophetic addresses to Ahaz in Isa 7 which we will consider in Chapter III.

This text, then, introduces a new point into the discussion. Not only does the particular setting of war determine how the conventional language of war is formulated but also the particular interests and thoughts of a specific "author" will influence the structure of speech.

Two concluding observations can be made: (1) Isaiah, who speaks out of the royal/Zion theological tradition, appropriates the same conventional formulaic elements as those found in the typical Deuteronomic texts. (2) The use of conventional language of war, however, is altered by the theological persuasion of the "author." Isaiah does not use Orders to give instruction to warriors who will participate in the battle but speaks of the Promise of Yahweh's intervention. Yahweh will fight alone against the enemy to give

Hezekiah the victory. The different theological tradition reflected in this text, then, is suggestive of the fact that the conventional language of war we have been analyzing in the Deuteronomic corpus is typical of other than Deuteronomic literary traditions as well.

The Conventional Language of War in Larger Narrative Contexts

Still other passages in the Deuteronomic History need to be considered. The elements of the conventional language of war characteristically present in shorter utterances like those we have considered thus far are typically present in texts scattered throughout a larger narrative, even where the shorter utterance is not present. Following is an analysis of these remaining "fear not" texts in the Deuteronomic History connected with war settings.

l.   *2 Kgs l:l-l6*

This passage presents us with still another setting in which the conventional elements of the language of war occur. Here Yahweh addresses Elijah, a war prophet. As we will see below, other prophets such as Jeremiah are war prophets and are addressed with language typically associated with the conduct of war. As prophets of the divine warrior, Yahweh, they carry out their orders, i.e., they speak oracles of judgment and destruction against the king and the people. In 2 Kgs 1:1-16 Elijah is ordered to be part of Yahweh's offense and to attack Ahaziah, the king, with words of judgment pronouncing the king's imminent death for having sought oracular information from Baal-zebub, the god of Ekron, rather than from Yahweh. Yahweh takes an offensive action against Ahaziah, giving Elijah the following directive,

> Arise, go up to meet the messengers of the king of Samaria, and say
> to them, "Is it because there is no God in Israel that you are going to
> inquire of Baal-zebub, the god of Ekron?" Now therefore thus says
> the LORD, "You shall not come down from the bed to which you have
> gone, but you shall surely die."
>
> קום עלה לקראת מלאכי מלך שמרון ודבר אלהם המבלי אין אלהים בישראל
> אתם הלכים לדרש בבעל זבוב אלהי עקרון ולכן כה אמר יהוה המטה
> אשר עלית שם לא תרד ממנה

> —2 Kgs 1:3b-4

Notice here how the imperatives קום and עלה which introduce the Directive are precisely the same as those in Josh 8:1-2. (See also the use of עלה in Deut 1:20-21.) The close relationship between the Directive and the Orders which we noted in our discussion of Josh 8:1-2 is to be seen here in that the Directive contains Elijah's orders, i.e., the specific words Elijah is to speak.

Elijah obeys this Directive and carries out his orders as is clear from vss. 5-6 where the messengers of the king report that Elijah spoke to them words identical to those he was ordered to speak.

The war connotations of this whole affair are strengthened by the response the king makes to the oracle. He repeatedly sends military troops ("one captain of fifty with his fifty") to seize Elijah. Each time until the last captain comes, the captain is killed by fire that comes down from heaven which consumes him. When the last captain begs mercy from Elijah (vs. 13), Yahweh addresses Elijah with additional formulaic language used to address warriors (vs. 15):

    (a)   DIRECTIVE

        Go down with him;
        רד אותו

    (b)   ASSURANCE

        do not fear
        אל תירא

    (c)   OBJECT OF FEAR

        him.
        מפניו

The use of the Object of Fear shows that Elijah, who had originally made an offensive attack, is now put in a defensive situation by the counter-attack of the king. However, after Yahweh addresses Elijah, his prophetic warrior, Elijah immediately obeys the Directive and follows his orders to speak the words given him earlier. The speaking of the divine oracle, i.e., the carrying out of the orders of this prophetic warrior, has the same devastating consequences we noted in the earlier texts we considered. Immediately after Elijah carries out his orders and speaks the oracle, we are told simply, "So he (Ahaziah) died" (1:17). The prophet has carried out his military orders from the divine warrior and wins the offensive battle with the king.

Here, then, the conventional language of war is used not to address a military warrior of Yahweh but a prophetic warrior. That Elijah is pictured as a war prophet here

is consistent with other presentations of Elijah as a prophet of war, e.g., when he rides
the military horses and chariots of fire into heaven (2 Kgs 2:11). Most of the typical
formulaic elements of war language appear here although they are scattered throughout
the narrative. There is no Basis of Assurance. However, the fire from heaven which
repeatedly consumes the military envoys is a gestural equivalent—a concrete expression
of assurance to a prophetic warrior of Yahweh.

2.   *2 Kgs 6:8-23*

The language of address to a warrior in this chapter also is scattered throughout the
passage, which concerns an unnamed Assyrian king and an unknown Israelite king. The
opening verses of the narrative (vss. 8-10) state how Elisha was accustomed to inform the
king of Israel about the military maneuvers of enemy kings. The Syrian king mentioned
in this passage became frustrated that his military maneuvers were always being
discovered by the king of Israel, and he concluded that there might be an informant in his
entourage (vs. 11). When the Syrian king is told that it is not an informant but the
prophet Elisha who tells the Syrian's plans to the Israelite king (vs. 12), the Syrian king
sends a great army with chariots and horses to surround the city where Elisha is and to
seize him. In the early morning a servant of Elisha awakes and is distressed by the great
army which had surrounded the city during the night. The servant asks Elisha, "Alas, my
master! What shall we do (vs. 15)?" Elisha responds with language characteristic of war
in vs. 16:

    (a)   ASSURANCE

        Fear not,
        אל תירא

    (b)   BASIS OF ASSURANCE

        for those who are with us are more than those who are with them.
        כי רבים אשר אתנו מאשר אתם

Here are two formulaic elements characteristically occurring in the language of war:
the Assurance and the Basis of Assurance. Notice that the Basis of Assurance is
introduced typically by the particle כי. The Basis of Assurance also alludes to the
presence of a superior force "with us" (אתנו), a motif typically found in the Basis of
Assurance, e.g., Deut 20:3-4 and 31:6.

That Elisha is referring to Yahweh and his heavenly army is evident from the ensuing verses which introduce another element typical of the language of war. Elisha prays to Yahweh,

> O LORD, I pray thee, open his eyes (i.e., the eyes of Elisha's servant)
> that he may see.
>
> יהוה פקח נא את עיניו ויראה
>
> —2 Kgs 6:17

It will be recalled that the Basis of Assurance in war speech may be introduced not by the particle כי, but by the imperative ראה, "see." For example, in Josh 8:1-2, "see (ראה) I have given into your hand the king of Ai, and his people and his city, and his land;" and in Deut 1:21, "see (ראה) the LORD your God has set the land before you." Elisha's prayer is a request that his servant might see (ראה) because seeing will be a basis of the Assurance not to fear. The following verses make it clear that the servant does see and is assured.

> So the LORD opened the eyes of the young man, and he saw (וירא);
> and behold (והנה), the mountain was full of horses and chariots of
> fire round about Elisha.
>
> —2 Kgs 6:17

It will be recalled that הנה has also been used to introduce a Basis of Assurance (see 2 Kgs 19:6//Isa 37:6).

It is not necessary for us to consider the rest of this account which tells how the king of Israel through divine intervention gained the upper hand in the battle and how the Syrians were sent away in peace and came no more to raid Israel. It is important to observe, however, that while there is no short utterance here, formulaic elements typical of the language of war do emerge in this war narrative.

3.   The Formula "Fear not" in Two Remaining Texts with War Settings

There are two other places in the Deuteronomic History where "Fear not" occurs in a short phrase of comfort addressed to one who is frightened by the terrors of war. In Judg 4:18 Jael says to Sisera in flight from Barak who had routed all his chariots and his army, "Turn aside, my lord, turn aside to me; have no fear" (אל תירא); and in 1 Sam 22:2 David says to Abiathar, fleeing for his life from the massacre of the priests of Nob, "Stay with me, fear not (אל תירא); for he that seeks my life seeks your life; with me you shall be in safekeeping."

These two passages make it clear that "fear not" is a phrase used primarily as an expression of assurance addressed to a person experiencing the terrors of war. However, that does not mean that the phrase "fear not" has become a technical term preserved solely for usage in a war setting. This phrase can be and is used in the Deuteronomic History as words of assurance in other situations as well. Thus Saul comforts the witch of Endor (1 Sam 28:13), Elijah comforts the widow of Zarephath (1 Kgs 17:13), and the wife of Phineas is comforted by the women attending her at childbirth (1 Sam 4:20).

Fear Not and the Conventional Language of War: A Summary

It has been the purpose of this chapter to survey the "fear not" pericopes in war settings in the Deuteronomic History. Our investigation has shown that the phrase, "fear not," is a key component in conventional language of war. This is not to say that the very occurrence of the phrase suggests the connotations of war to the reader of the text. But the term does occur in the Deuteronomic History most frequently in textual settings associated with the conduct of war. It is used most often to comfort a warrior before a military campaign. The use of the phrase in situations concerning an impending battle has been extended so that it becomes an appropriate form of expression to comfort an individual who has become caught up in the terror and ravages of war.

Furthermore, in the Deuteronomic History "fear not" is used in conjunction with other regularly occurring formulaic elements so that it is possible to speak of a conventional or stereotypical way of constructing the language of a speaker addressing a warrior who faces an impending battle or who faces the general prospect of war. This conventional use of language can be extended to other situations as well, e.g., in offering refuge to a defeated enemy (David speaking to Mephibosheth) or in conceding the throne to a contender (Jonathan to David). We also showed that the conventional structure for the language of war was typical of both divine speech and human speech, i.e., it is typical of war generally and cannot be used to point to a particular practice of war such as the supposed institution of holy war associated with the twelve tribe league. We also hinted that this conventional use of language to address a warrior was not merely a Deuteronomic convention but was a much more general convention occurring in other literary traditions, e.g., in the prophetic war oracle of Isaiah. The remaining chapters in the book examine other literary corpora of material to demonstrate this thesis.

The elements that we have identified with "fear not" in the conventional language of war are as follows:

1.   *Assurance*—This is the phrase "fear not" (אל תירא or its plural equivalent
אל תיראו). In the Deuteronomic History it frequently occurs at the beginning of a text
containing the language of war. Sometimes it attracts similar words of assurance,
especially in those texts concerned with exhortation, e.g., offensive war situations in
Josh 8:1-2 and Deut 1:20-21 which add the phrase ואל תחת ("do not be dismayed").
Similarly, the priestly oracle in Deut 20:3-4 designed to rally the troops expands the
element significantly, אל ירך לבבכם אל תיראו ואל תחפזו ואל תערצו ("let not your heart
faint, do not fear, or tremble, or be in dread").

2.   *Encouragement*—This is the imperative חזק or the imperative phrase חזק ואמץ
חזקו והיו לבבי חיל in 2 Sam 13:28). It is often closely associated with the Assurance
but has the particular purpose of encouraging a warrior who has been given a new and
responsible task in a battle.

3.   *Object of Fear*—This element, which is characteristic of defensive situations,
nearly always follows the Assurance and refers to the enemy which is the source of
fear. It is formulated typically with מן or מפני. (See את in Deut 3:2//Num 21:34).

4.   *Basis of Assurance*—This element states the reason that the warrior need not
be afraid. It is, therefore, usually introduced with the particle כי ("because, for") but, in
offensive situations, it is characteristically introduced with the imperative ראה ("see") or
by the particle הנה ("behold"). It is usually formulated in the first person singular where
the one speaking gives his reason that there should be no fear. In divine speech the
recurring phrase is "I (Yahweh) have given (נתתי) someone into your hand" (בידך). In the
general prospect of war the deity is referred to as "the one who goes with you" (ההלך
עמך/אתך), see Deut 20:3-4 and 31:6. The formulation of this element, however, is
somewhat fluid. It typically follows the Assurance although it will follow the Object of
Fear when that element occurs.

5.   *Orders*—This is typically formulated in the second person and gives the orders
to be carried out in an ensuing battle. It occurs, then, only when an ensuing battle is
imminent and not when the prospect of war generally is envisaged.

6.   *Directive*—This is characteristic of an offensive situation and usually occurs
both near the beginning and at the end of the address to a warrior. It is formulated with
imperative verbs. The first Directive is to initiate a battle and the imperatives קום
and עלה are frequently used. The second Directive usually concerns the carrying out of

specific orders for the battle. The Directive is closely related to the Orders; however, in offensive situations it serves as an exhortation to initiate a battle.

7.   *Promise*—This can be rather free in its formulation and occurs usually when there is the general prospect of war. A text promises that the general outcome of a military threat will be favorable. In the Isaiah oracle we referred to a Promise. As we will see in Isaiah's theological tradition, only Yahweh fights and there are no specific battle orders to be carried out. The Promise is an alternative to Orders used when Yahweh himself does the fighting or when war is a general or hypothetical rather than a specific or imminent concern.

8.   In addition to these regularly recurring formulaic elements in the conventional patterning of the language of war we also noted other elements that occurred only once or twice as specific situations demanded—the Summons to Hear, the Address and the Prophetic Messenger Formula.

We are arguing that all of these elements occur regularly with the phrase "fear not" and constitute what we have called the conventional language of war. They are the typical components used by an "author" in constructing the words of someone who is addressing a warrior before a specific battle or concerning the general prospect of war. It would not be particularly helpful to construct an ideal model from the recurring elements and argue that it was a *Gattung* with its *Sitz im Leben* in war. No ideal form ever existed, but there were conventional or stereotypical ways of constructing the language of address to a warrior. Furthermore, it is possible to classify typical situations of war and the typical elements used in structuring the language as follows:

1.   *Defensive situations*

    a.   Assurance
    b.   Objective of Fear
    c.   Basis of Assurance
    d.   Orders

2.   *Offensive situations*

    a.   Assurance
    b.   Directive
    c.   Basis of Assurance
    d.   Orders
    e.   Directive (or concluding Assurance)

3.   *General Prospect of War*

    a.   Assurance
    b.   Object of Fear

      c.   Basis of Assurance
      d.   Promise

4.   *New task for the warrior*

      a.   Encouragement
      b.   Elements associated with defense, offense or the general prospect of war.

It is important to realize, however, that any classification a scholar imposes upon the material will never adequately reflect each situation. The classification exists as a tool to help identify the conventional language of war. Such a classification never existed in ancient Israel to recommend ideal types to be followed rigidly by an "author" or "speaker." The actual construction of a particular address to a warrior, while making use of the conventions of language of war, will vary depending on the specific situation and the particular interests or intentions of the "speaker" or "author."

CHAPTER II

"FEAR NOT" AND THE PROPHETIC WARRIOR

Introduction

In the last chapter we argued that, in the Deuteronomic History, conventional language used to address a warrior was employed in divine speech when Yahweh addressed his servants as warriors. We suggested that Yahweh's warriors were of two kinds: those who, like Joshua, were warriors of Yahweh in the conventional sense of being actively involved in war following the orders of Yahweh to fight and those, who like Elijah, were prophetic warriors of Yahweh given orders by Yahweh to be actively engaged in the battle against the enemy but whose weapons were not the ordinary instruments of war; Elijah was to attack the enemy by delivering Yahweh's words. This chapter will focus on the prophet Jeremiah who among the classical prophets most clearly represents a prophetic warrior of Yahweh. The chapter will be concentrated mainly on the call of Jeremiah (Jer 1:14-19)[1] where Yahweh addresses Jeremiah as a prophetic warrior in a prelude to the war of words which follows in the book. The chapter will also consider Jer 42:17ff., a passage where Jeremiah addresses warriors in a way reminiscent of Gedaliah's address (see above, pp. 19-21).

The Call of Jeremiah (Jer 1:4-19)

Form critical studies have been primarily concerned with the call of Jeremiah in 1:4-10. Some have sought to show that these verses conform to a call *Gattung* that governs other call narratives in the Hebrew Scriptures.[2] Others have focused on the so-called Oracle of Salvation in vs. 8 as a clue to understanding Jeremiah's call either as a liturgical ritual[3] or as a clue to the unique form of Jeremiah's call.[4] Two major questions related to these form critical matters have been raised by scholars. (1) How does the call of Jeremiah in Jer 1:4-10 relate to the rest of the chapter, i.e., to the two visions in Jer 1:11ff. and 1:13ff. as well as to the other so-called Oracle of Salvation in Jer 1:17ff.?[5] (2) How is one to explain the close relation between the commission of Jeremiah in Jer 1:7 and the figure of Moses in Deut 18:18?[6]

Our analysis of this chapter will make an alternative suggestion concerning the form critical analysis of the text and will consider the two related questions. On the one hand we cannot agree with those who hold that the so-called Oracle of Salvation is employed in Jeremiah's call. As we have argued, the formula "fear not" is not typical of the so-called Oracle of Salvation. It is, rather, typical of the conventional language used to address a warrior which, as we have seen in the Deuteronomic History, is adapted as a form of address to a prophetic warrior. On the other hand we cannot agree with those who explain this chapter simply as representative of the call *Gattung*. Such an analysis does not do justice to the formula "fear not" and the other elements in the conventional language of war which occur in this chapter. Indeed, we will argue that most of the chapter can be understood as employing the conventional language used to address a warrior. The relation of Jeremiah to Moses and other "servants" of Yahweh in the Deuteronomic History is that the language used to address warriors in both places is drawn from the conventional language associated with war. Whether the similarities to the Deuteronomic History are due to a Deuteronomic redaction of the material in Jer 1 is not a question we wish to pursue. However, our observation about the text of Jer 1, as it now stands, has important implications for those who wish to pursue the question of the redaction of the book.

To facilitate specific analysis of the use of conventional language to address a warrior in Jer 1, we will first discuss in summary the overall structure of the chapter.[7] After the opening superscription (1:1-3), the account of Jeremiah's call is introduced by the formula, "Now the word of the LORD came to me saying" (ויהי דבר יהוה אלי לאמר), a formula that occurs also in vss. 11, 13 and 2:1.[8] In vs. 5 Jeremiah is commissioned by Yahweh to be a "prophet to the nations," and in vs. 6 Jeremiah objects to that commissioning.[9] In vss. 7-19, which draw particularly on the conventional language of war, it becomes apparent that Jeremiah's vocation as a prophet to the nations is that of a prophetic warrior. In vss. 7-19 Jeremiah is addressed twice as a warrior: (1) In vss. 7-8 Yahweh speaks to Jeremiah generally concerning his future as one whose vocation is that of prophetic warrior against the nations. (2) In vss. 17-19 Yahweh speaks to Jeremiah concerning the specific war Jeremiah is to wage against Jerusalem and the cities of Judah. The intervening material (which includes the two visions in vss. 11ff. and vss. 13ff.) serve as a transition from Yahweh's comforting of Jeremiah in his general task as a prophetic warrior to his comforting of Jeremiah in his specific task as a prophetic warrior against Judah.

The structure of vss. 7-8 can be outlined as follows:

(a)   DIRECTIVE

> Do not say, "I am only a youth;"
>
> אל תאמר נער אנכי

(b)   ORDERS

> for to all to whom I send you you shall go, and whatever I command you you shall speak.
>
> כי על כל אשר אשלחך תלך ואת כל אשר אצוך תדבר

(c)   ASSURANCE

> Be not afraid
>
> אל ותירא

(d)   OBJECT OF FEAR

> of them,
>
> מפניהם

(e)   BASIS OF ASSURANCE

> for I am with you
>
> כי אתך אני

(f)   PROMISE

> to deliver you,
>
> להצלך

(g)   PROPHETIC FORMULA

> says the LORD.
>
> נאם יהוה

The Directives we have considered thus far have been positive imperative commands regarding specific instructions for an offensive battle. Here the formulation of the Directive has been slightly altered to fit the context of the passage. It is a negative command (אל תאמר נער אנכי) which is a response to the objection of Jeremiah (1:6) to his commission as a prophetic warrior (1:5). The Directive here does not concern a specific battle but the commission of Jeremiah to his new vocation as an offensive prophetic warrior against the nations.

The Orders are formulated similarly to those we have considered earlier. They are in the second person giving instructions for the coming battle. They are general in nature because they do not concern a specific battle for the prophet but the general prospect of war. The close relationship of these Orders to the Orders given to Israel in Deut 31:5 when Israel faced the general prospect of a war of conquest is striking. In Deut 31:5 Israel is ordered, "you will do (ועשיתם) to them according to all the commandment which I have commanded you (צויתי)." Jeremiah is ordered, "all which I command you (אצוך) you will speak (תדבר)." These Orders make it clear also that Jeremiah is not a conventional warrior who fights with weapons; he is to fight by speaking Yahweh's words. The introduction of the Orders by the particle כי is uncommon, but here the Orders given Jeremiah are related to the Directive.

The Assurance is the typical אל תירא and the Object of Fear is typically constructed with מפני. The Basis of Assurance is introduced by the expected particle כי and like other Bases of Assurance in general war situations contains the motif of Yahweh's being "with you" (cf. Deut 20:3-4 and 31:5-6).

The Promise announces what can be generally expected, and here the Promise formulated with the infinitive (להצלך) is similar to the Promise in Deut 20:4 formulated with the infinitive (להלחם לכם עם איביכם להושיע אתכם).

The language Yahweh uses to address Jeremiah in vss. 7-8, then, employs the conventional elements used to address warriors in the Deuteronomic History. Not just vss. 7-8 but the remainder of the chapter suggest the situation of war as the background for understanding the call of Jeremiah to his vocation as a war prophet.

The Orders given to Jeremiah in vs. 7 are that he is to go to whomever Yahweh sent him and to speak whatever Yahweh commanded him. Immediately after addressing the prophetic warrior (vss. 7-8), Yahweh puts forth his hand, touches Jeremiah's lips and thereby gives Jeremiah the ammunition ("Behold, I have put my words in your mouth," vs. 9) for carrying out his orders to speak as a prophetic warrior. While there is nothing quite comparable to this action in any of the pericopes we have considered in the Deuteronomic History (but compare Josh 10:24-26), the words of Yahweh have similarities to the structural element that we have called the Basis of Assurance. Yahweh's words are introduced by the particle, הנה, as is the Basis of Assurance in 2 Kgs 19:6//Isa 37:6. This particle signals the transition to seeing, the new theme being introduced into the chapter. The next verse (vs. 10) introduces an additional Basis of Assurance to Jeremiah introduced by the imperative ראה.

> See (ראה), I have set you this day over
> nations and kingdoms,
> to pluck up and to break down,
> to destroy and to overthrow,
> to build and to plant.

We have argued that in offensive situations the Basis of Assurance is customarily introduced by the imperative ראה (cf. Josh 8:1-2 and Deut 1:20-21). Jeremiah can be assured of his success as a warrior "prophet to the nations" because Yahweh has placed his words in Jeremiah's mouth and has commanded Jeremiah to see that Yahweh has set him (הפקדתיך) over nations and kingdoms.

We will return below to a full discussion of the assurance offered to Jeremiah in vs. 10 and the commission of Jeremiah in vs. 5. It is important now, however, to pursue the importance of "seeing" (ראה) in this chapter. The emphasis on "seeing" as a confirmation of victory was particulary important in the Deuteronomic History when Yahweh spoke to warriors (cf. Josh 8:1-2; Deut 1:20-21 and 2 Kgs 19:6//Isa 37:6). It will be recalled that this was stressed in the passage where the prophet Elisha prayed that his servant could see and thus be assured of victory.

> O, LORD, I pray thee, open his eyes that he may see (ויראה).
>
> —2 Kgs 6:17

Yahweh subsequently opened the eyes of the servant, who was assured when he saw the heavenly army.

> So the LORD opened the eyes of the young man, and he saw (וירא);
> and behold (והנה), the mountain was full of horses and chariots of
> fire round about.
>
> —2 Kgs 6:17

It is our contention that the visions (1:11f. and 1:13f.) in their present setting perform this same function. They open Jeremiah's eyes so that he can see and be asssured of his success as a warrior.

In the first vision Yahweh says to Jeremiah, "What do you see (מה אתה ראה)? Jeremiah responds, "I see a rod of almond (שקד אני ראה)." This vision serves to assure Jeremiah of success in his vocation as a prophetic warrior speaking the words of Yahweh placed in his mouth. Yahweh's explanation of the meaning of the vision, "You have seen well (היטבת לראות) for I am watching (שקד) over my word (דבר) to perform it (vs. 9), "refers to the Orders given to Jeremiah in vs. 7 to speak for Yahweh and to vs. 9 where Yahweh assures Jeremiah that he, Yahweh, has placed his words in Jeremiah's mouth. This first vision, then, functions to assure Jeremiah in his general vocation of prophetic warrior.

The second vision in vs. 13f. is introduced by the formula, "The word of the LORD came to me a second time saying (ויהי דבר יהוה אלי שנית לאמר)." The use of the word שנית (second) has been baffling to scholars. This is the third time the formula has been used in this chapter; it is used also in 1:4 and 1:11. One would expect the formula to read "a third time" (שלישית), if it is numbered at all.[10] Our contention, however, is that the word שנית does not simply enumerate a formula used in this chapter. It numbers the second vision and is a key to the second address to Jeremiah as a warrior in vss. 17-19 and to the structure of the chapter. The first vision assures Jeremiah in his general commission to be a prophetic warrior; the second vision assures Jeremiah in his specific role as a prophetic warrior against Judah. The first vision follows the first address to Jeremiah; the second vision precedes the second address. The conventional language of war has been utilized to form a chiasmic structure[11] in the chapter, following the commissioning of Jeremiah in vs. 5 and Jeremiah's objection in vs. 6. The structure a b c, c' b' a' can be outlined as follows:

a. Address to Jeremiah
as general warrior
(vss. 7-8)

   b. Yahweh's actions
   giving assurance
   (vss. 9-10)

      c. Vision giving assurance
      (vss. 11-12)

      c'. Vision giving assurance
      (vss. 13-14)

   b'. Yahweh's actions
   giving assurance
   (vss. 15-16)

a'. Address to Jeremiah
as warrior against
Judah
(vss. 17-19)

Here our form critical inquiry has not led us away from the final form of the text but has
given us insight into the rhetorical features of the text in its final form. We have
analyzed the first three elements of this chiasmic structure (a, b, c); we now need to look
at the last three elements of the structure (c', b', a'). The second vision following the
introductory formula is similar in structure to the first vision. As in this first vision,
Yahweh asks Jeremiah, 'What do you see (מה אתה ראה)?" Jeremiah's response resembles
his response to the first vision, "I see (אני ראה) a boiling pot facing away from the
north." Just as Yahweh had explained the meaning of the first vision (vs. 12), so Yahweh
now explains the meaning of this vision to Jeremiah (vs. 14). In both places the
explanation is introduced by the same words, "Then the LORD said to me"
(ויאמר יהוה אלי). Here the explanation of the vision of the boiling pot is, "Out of the
north evil shall break forth upon all the inhabitants of the land." The explanation of this
vision refers to the judgment Yahweh will bring against Judah. It gives assurance to
Jeremiah as he faces his task as a prophetic warrior carrying out a specific campaign
against Judah, and it parallels the first vision which assured Jeremiah in his general
vocation as a prophetic warrior.

Vss. 15-16 emphasize the action of Yahweh just as did vss. 9-10. We argued that vss.
9-10 were formulated as the Basis of Assurance, a typical element in the language of
war. Similarly vss. 15-16 are introduced by two particles characteristic of the Basis of
Assurance (הנה and כי).

> For (כי), behold I (הנני) am calling all the tribes of the kingdoms of
> the north, says the LORD; and they shall come and every one shall
> set his throne at the entrance of the gates of Jerusalem, against all
> the cities of Judah. And I will utter my judgments against them, for
> all their wickedness in forsaking me; they have burned incense to
> other gods, and worshipped the works of their own hands.

Just as the first vision in vss. 11-12 had strengthened Yahweh's preceding assurance (vss.
9-10) that he would put his words in Jeremiah's mouth, so the second vision strengthens
Yahweh's subsequent assurance that he will bring judgment against Judah. The assurance
in vss. 15-16 leads into Yahweh's second address to Jeremiah (vss. 17-19) concerning his
campaign against Judah.

Yahweh's second address to Jeremiah as a warrior can be outlined as follows:

(a)   ORDERS

But you, gird up your loins; arise,
and say to them everything that I
command you.
ואתה תאזר מתניך וקמת ודברת
אליהם את כל אשר אנכי אצוך

(b)   ASSURANCE

Do not be dismayed
אל תחת

(c)   OBJECT OF FEAR

by them,
מפניהם

(d)   BASIS OF ASSURANCE

(lest I dismay you before them.)   And I, behold, I make you this day a
fortified city, an iron pillar, and bronze walls against the whole land, against
the kings of Judah, its princes, its priests, and the people of the land.
(פן אחתך לפניהם) ואני הנה נתתיך היום לעיר מבצר ולעמוד ברזל ולחמות
נחשת על כל הארץ למלכי יהודה לשריה לכהניה ולעם הארץ

(e)   PROMISE

They will fight against you; but they shall not prevail against you,
ונלחמו אליך ולא יוכלו לך

(f)   BASIS OF ASSURANCE

for I am with you,
כי אתך אני

(g)   PROPHETIC FORMULA

says the LORD,
נאם יהוה

(h)   PROMISE

to deliver you.
להצילך

This address to Jeremiah is specifically concerned with the role of the prophetic
warrior battling against Judah.[12] It has some of the elements that we have associated
with offensive war and some of the elements that we have associated with defensive
war. The Orders here use some of the vocabulary of the Directive typical of offensive
situations such as the word קום.[13]   The Directive normally uses the imperative.
However, that is not the case here. In this campaign against Judah, Jeremiah is to fight
as he was ordered to do in the opening address concerning Jeremiah's general vocation as

prophetic warrior. He is to speak everything which Yahweh commands him. The Orders
suggest an offensive campaign against Judah.

The Assurance is not the usual אל תירא but אל תחת, a phrase we have encountered
above in combination with אל תירא (cf. Josh 8:1-2; Deut 1:20-21 and 31:7-8). The Object
of Fear, characteristic of defensive war settings, is formulated as expected with מפני.
However, the words "lest I dismay you before them," is not typical of the words of
address to a warrior that we have considered thus far. It is a threat and is reminiscent of
the sometimes less than comforting words Yahweh speaks to Jeremiah in response to
Jeremiah's confessions (cf. 15:19-21). These words are an indication that the *Gattung* is
adapted to its use in Jeremiah and conforms to the peculiarities of that book.

The Basis of Assurance is introduced with the pronoun אני and the particle הנה, a
particle sometimes used with the Basis of Assurance (cf. 2 Kgs 19:6//Isa 37:6 and Jer
1:9). The word נתן is also used, but here the accomplished fact does not concern the
enemy being given into the hand of the warrior but concerns Yahweh making Jeremiah
invincible against the enemy.

The pericope ends with elements drawn from the language typical of address to a
warrior facing the general prospect of war. There is a Promise, "They shall fight against
you; but they shall not prevail against you," announcing the general outcome (cf. Deut
31:5-6 and 7-8). The Basis of Assurance, "for I am with you," is typical of situations in
which war is a general prospect (cf. Deut 20:3-4; 31:5-6 and Jer 1:8), as is the concluding
Promise with the infinitive (cf. Deut 20:4 and Jer 1:8).

On the basis of this form-critical investigation, it appears that much of the first
chapter of Jeremiah is to be understood against the background of war. This is
particularly true of the addresses to Jeremiah in vss. 7-8 and in vss. 17-19. Both
pericopes contain the conventional language typically used to address a warrior. This
form-critical insight has helped uncover the rhetorical features of the text itself. The
text moves in a chiasmic structure after the commissioning of Jeremiah from an address
to Jeremiah as a prophetic warrior in general to an address to Jeremiah as a specific
warrior against Judah.

While Jer 1:4-10 contains some features in common with other call narratives, as
Habel and Kutsch have argued,[14] it would be wrong to understand these verses simply as
an example of a call *Gattung*. Such an explanation would fail to deal adequately with the

conventions of war reflected in these verses. It would also fail to deal adequately with the relationship of these verses to the larger rhetorical unit comprising the rest of the chapter.

The realization that Jeremiah's call picks up the conventions of the language of war gives us insight into another problem recently raised by R.P. Carroll in his book, *From Chaos to Covenant.*[15] In his discussion of the call of Jeremiah Carroll asks,

> Whatever the formal elements of a call narrative may be, in determining its *Gestalt* it is important to relate the story to its context. Where does it appear in the tradition? What precedes or follows it? Can the editor's intention be discerned by the answers to such questions? For the placing of the call narrative and its context are important elements in the building up of the tradition and are also further variations in the pattern of the call genre.[16]

We would argue that the war connotations of Jeremiah's call provide a clue to the answer to these questions for the book of Jeremiah. The call of Jeremiah comes at the beginning of the book because Jeremiah is addressed as a warrior. The address to a warrior is conventional language spoken before a battle or before the general prospect of war; it does not occur in the midst of battle. The positioning of these words of address to Jeremiah before Jeremiah follows his orders and unleashes Yahweh's words of judgment on Judah and the nations is appropriate for the call of Jeremiah. In the call Yahweh comforts Jeremiah, his prophetic warrior, before the war fought with words which follows in the rest of the book. Whereas it is not necessary for Isaiah's call to be at the front of his book because Isaiah is not addressed as a prophetic warrior, it makes good sense for Jeremiah's call to be at the beginning of the book, because Jeremiah is addressed as a prophetic warrior.

That Jeremiah should be addressed as a warrior against the nations in general and against Judah in particular is consistent with the imagery which follows in the rest of the book. While we cannot investigate that imagery in detail, a few things can be said to indicate how the war imagery in Jeremiah's call relates to the persistent theme of Yahweh as warrior and Jeremiah as his warrior spokesman. For example, in Jer 25:15-16 Yahweh says to Jeremiah,

> Take from my hand this cup of the wine of wrath, and make all the nations to whom I send you drink it. They shall drink and stagger and be crazed because of the sword which I am sending among them.

Here the imperative (קַח) is reminiscent of the Directive and the phrase (את אתו והשקיתה

(כל הגוים אשר אנכי שלח אותך אליהם) is similar to the phrase (על כל אשר אשלחך תלך

(ואת כל אשר אצוך תדבר) in the original orders given to Jeremiah in Jer 1:7. Jeremiah

obeys the orders,

> So I took the cup from the LORD's hand, and made all the nations to
> whom the Lord sent me drink it.
>
> —Jer 25:17

Jerusalem and the cities of Judah are the first mentioned in the list of nations to receive

judgment from the cup, i.e., the sword of Yahweh. The devastating battle of Yahweh

against the nations is recorded in vs. 33,

> And those slain by the LORD on that day shall extend from one end
> of the earth to the other. They shall not be lamented, or gathered or
> buried; they shall be dung on the surface of the earth.

Other passages in Jeremiah present Jeremiah as the warrior spokesman of Yahweh, e.g.,

those passages where Jeremiah speaks of the foe from the north bringing destruction (see

4:5ff.; 5:15ff.; 6:1ff.; etc.). In these passages Jeremiah proclaims the coming of the foe

which he saw in the vision (1:13-14) during his call. In an answer to Yahweh to one of

Jeremiah's laments (Jer 15:19-21), many of the motifs of Yahweh's address to Jeremiah

as a warrior in 1:17-19 are picked up. This is especially true of vs. 20,

> And I will make you to this people
> a fortified wall of bronze;
> they will fight against you,
> but they shall not prevail over you,
> for I am with you
> to save and deliver you,
> says the LORD.

In short, the use of the conventional language of war in the call of Jeremiah is not

strange but is consistent with one of the major themes of the book, i.e., Jeremiah as the

warrior spokesman of Yahweh.[17]

Jeremiah as Yahweh's Governor (Jer 42)

The incident in Jer 42 gives us additional information about Jeremiah as a prophetic

warrior of Yahweh. In this chapter Yahweh does not address Jeremiah as a warrior;

rather it is Jeremiah who speaks to "the commanders of the forces" (שרי החילים) and the persons gathered with them after Gedaliah's assassination. Here Jeremiah's words in Jer

42:9ff. follow the supplication of the people to intercede with Yahweh on their behalf.

The message which Jeremiah delivers from Yahweh is a long address, and it is only the

beginning of the message (42:9-11) that follows the conventional language used to address

a warrior. The structure of these words is outlined as follows:

(a)   PROPHETIC FORMULA

>   Thus says the LORD, the God Israel, to whom you sent me to present your
>   supplication before him:
>
>   כה אמר יהוה אלהי ישראל אשר שלחתם אתי אליו להפיל תחנתכם לפניו

(b)   ORDERS

>   If you will remain in this land, then I will build you up and not pull you down;
>   I will plant you, and not pluck you up; for I repent of the evil which I did to
>   you.
>
>   אם שוב תשבו בארץ הזות ובניתי אתכם ולא אהרס ונטעתי אתכם ולא אהוש כי
>   נחמתי אל הרעה אשר עשיתי לכם

(c)   ASSURANCE

>   Do not fear
>   אל תיראו

(d)   OBJECT OF FEAR

>   the king of Babylon, of whom you are afraid;
>   מפני מלך בבל אשר אתם יראים מפניו

(e)   ASSURANCE

>   do not fear
>   אל וגיראו

(f)   OBJECT OF FEAR

>   him,
>   ממנו

(g)   PROPHETIC FORMULA

>   says the LORD,
>   נאם יהוה

(h)   BASIS OF ASSURANCE

>   for I am with you.
>   כי אתכם אני

(i)   PROMISE

>   to save you and to deliver you from his hand.
>   להושיע אתכם ולהציל אונכם מידו

A short discussion of the structure will help to clarify how the address to a warrior

has been appropriated here in the speech of Jeremiah. The address is introduced by the common messenger formula and is followed by an Orders. The Orders are typically in the second person. The conditional nature of the sentences, while not typical of the language of war, is typical of Jeremiah's speech (cf. Jer 7:5-7). This suggests that the form is not followed rigidly but is adapted as speech suitable for the prophetic warrior Jeremiah. Closely related to the words spoken to Jeremiah in his call (Jer 1:10), the Orders command the recipients of the message to remain in the land *if* they expect to be restored. The repeated use of the Assurance and the Object of Fear adds emphasis to the Orders to remain in the land. The Basis of Assurance promising the presence of Yahweh "with" the warriors (cf. Deut 20:3-4; 31:5-6; Jer 1:8) and the Promise with the infinitive construction (cf. Deut 20:4; Jer 1:8, 19) are typical of situations in which there is a general prospect of war rather than a specific battle.

How are we to understand Jeremiah's use of the language of war in this situation? To answer that question we will need to recall what was said about Gedaliah in the last chapter. After the king of Babylon had made Gedaliah governor (הפקיד; Jer 40:5, 7, 11; 41:2, 10, 18; cf. 2 Kgs 25:23), "the commanders of the forces" came to Gedaliah (Jer 40:7; cf. 2 Kgs 25:23). These are the same commanders who later came to Jeremiah after Gedaliah's assassination. When Gedaliah spoke to these warriors, he utilized the conventional language of address to a warrior—not to comfort the forces before a battle but to order the forces to live in peaceful co-existence with the new ruling military regime. Gedaliah, who was made an overseer of a defeated nation, was attempting to rebuild in cooperation with the Babylonians, the ruling regime.

Gedaliah was the governor representing Babylonia, the earthly victor of the defeated nation. Jeremiah was the governor representing Yahweh, the heavenly victor of the defeated nation. In the call of Jeremiah, Yahweh says to Jeremiah,

> See, I have made you governor (הפקדתיך)[18]
> this day over nations and over kingdoms,
> to pluck up and to break down,
> to destroy and to overthrow,
> to build and to plant.
>
> —Jer 1:10

Here the same word (פקד) used to indicate Gedaliah's appointment as governor of Babylon is used to indicate Jeremiah's appointment as governor.

When Gedaliah in his position as governor addressed the warriors, he represented defeat at the hands of the Babylonians; but his words to the forces called for a rebuilding of the land.   As the governor of Yahweh, Jeremiah likewise represented not only destruction but also renewal.   When Jeremiah addressed the commanders of the forces in Jer 42, his orders to the forces reflect the language of his original appointment as governor.

> If you will remain in this land, then I will build (ובניתי) you up and not pull (אהרס) you down; I will plant (ונטעתי) you, and not pluck (אתוש) you up.

                                                              —Jer 42:10a

Here the words הרס, בנה, נטע and נתש repeat words used in Jer 1:10.   Rebuilding will result only when Judah accepts its new status as a defeated nation (cf. 42:14ff.).   This was essentially the meaning of Gedaliah's words spoken earlier before his assassination.

The words spoken by Jeremiah in 42:9-11 as well as those spoken to Jeremiah in Jer 1:10 indicate that one of the roles of Jeremiah as a prophetic warrior of Yahweh was parallel to that of Gedaliah, who was appointed as the representative of the victor to begin reconstruction of the defeated nation.

Conclusion

In the book of Jeremiah, then, stereotypical language used to comfort a warrior is appropriated in the imaging of Jeremiah's prophetic vocation.   He is seen as an active warrior of Yahweh, like Moses and Joshua, who is given orders to actively fight for Yahweh.   Unlike the battles of Moses and Joshua, however, the war, which Yahweh is waging and in which Jeremiah is ordered to participate, is not against the enemies of Israel only but primarily against Yahweh's own people, the inhabitants of Judah.   Also, unlike Moses and Joshua, Jeremiah is ordered to fight not with conventional weapons as a conventional warrior but with the words of Yahweh who called him to be a prophetic warrior against the nations in general and against Judah in particular.

CHAPTER III

WAR ORACLES ADDRESSED TO KINGS

Introduction

In our discussion of the language of address to warriors in the Deuteronomic History and in Jeremiah we noted that in situations where a military attack was imminent, whether defensive or offensive, the warrior was given orders to be actively engaged with Yahweh in the fighting. This was true not only for conventional warriors such as Joshua who fought with weapons but also for the unconventional warrior Jeremiah who fought with words. The major exception to the use of the genre to convey orders in the face of military engagement was the oracle of Yahweh which Isaiah delivered to Hezekiah, the king of Judah, at the time of Sennacherib's invasion (2 Kgs 19:6//Isa 37:6).[1] In this situation Hezekiah was not given orders to be an active participant in the fighting, but he was given a promise that Yahweh himself would guarantee the defeat of Sennacherib in his own land where he would fall by the sword. In short, the king was not ordered to be actively engaged in battle but was to assume a passive role.[2]

In this chapter we will examine the war oracle which Isaiah delivered to King Ahaz (Isa 7:4-9) as well as some texts outside the biblical corpus where deities comfort kings facing the imminent prospect of war. While these texts follow the conventions of the language of address to a warrior, they do not give kings orders to be actively engaged with the deity in battle. They either promise the king that the deity will fight for him or give the king orders to take a passive role in the coming battle.

Our discussion will be developed in two significant ways in this chapter: (1) It will be shown that the stereotypical language of address to a warrior that we uncovered in the Deuteronomic History and the book of Jeremiah, which has for a long time been seen to be closely related to the Deuteronomic corpus,[3] is also typical of literature that has arisen in traditions independent of the Deuteronomic History, namely, in traditions associated with the prophet Isaiah. Furthermore, the chapter will demonstrate that this conventional language is also found in texts outside the Hebrew Scriptures that can be roughly dated in the same time period as Isaiah. (2) The other point that the chapter will begin to develop is that this stereotypical language is used in the Hebrew Scriptures to address two distinctive paradigmatic warriors of Yahweh. In the Deuteronomic corpus

52

and the book of Jeremiah Yahweh addresses warriors to whom he gives orders to be actively engaged in the battle with him. In the book of Isaiah the king is never given orders to be an active participant with Yahweh in battle. Yahweh will fight for the king, and if the king is given orders at all, he is ordered to play a passive role and to have confidence in the power of the deity who will fight for him. As we will see in subsequent chapters, the role of the royal warrior is assumed by the exilic community in Second Isaiah and in even later post-exilic texts. Joshua is the paradigmatic warrior in the Deuteronomic texts; the paradigmatic warrior for exilic and post-exilic texts is not David, as might be expected, but Abraham, the royal warrior and father of the community for whom Yahweh will fight to fulfill his promises.

Isa 7:4-9

In these verses Isaiah delivers an oracle to Ahaz concerning the military threat of the Syro-Ephraimite alliance. Apparently Pekah, the king of Ephraim, and Rezin, the king of Damascus, had formed an alliance in order to depose Ahaz from the Judean throne and to install a more favorable ruler who would be in sympathy with their scheme to gain independence from Assyria. They sought to do this by waging war against Jerusalem. It is in this context that Isaiah, as a prophet of Yahweh, speaks to Ahaz. He meets Ahaz "at the conduit of the upper pool on the highway to the Fuller's field" (Isa 7:3). That Ahaz was probably inspecting the water supply is an indication that he was making preparations for an expected battle.[4]

The words Isaiah uses to address Ahaz in this defensive military situation are similar to those he addressed to Hezekiah (2 Kgs 19:6//Isa 37:6) which we examined above. In both cases Isaiah is employing the stereotypical language of address to a warrior. The structure of Isa 7:4-9 can be outlined as follows:

(a)   DIRECTIVE

Take heed, be quiet,
השמר והשקט

(b)   ASSURANCE

do not fear, and do not let your heart be faint
אל תירא ולבבך אל ירך

(c)   OBJECT OF FEAR

> because of these two smoldering stumps of firebrands, at the fierce anger of
> Rezin and Syria and the son of Remaliah. Because Syria, with Ephraim and
> the son of Remaliah, has devised evil against you saying, "Let us go up
> against Judah and terrify it, and let us conquer it for ourselves, and set up
> the son of Tabeel as the king in the midst of it,"
>
> משני זנבות האודים העשנים האלה בחרי אף רצין וארם ובן רמליהו יען כי
> יעץ עליך ארם רעה אפרים ובן רמליהו לאמר נעלה ביהודה ונקיצנה ונבקענה
> אלינו ונמליך מלך בתוכה את בן טבאל

(d)   BASIS OF ASSURANCE

> thus says the LORD God:
> It shall not stand,
>   and it shall not come to pass.
> For the head of Syria is Damascus,
>   and the head of Damascus is Rezin.
> (Within sixty-five years Ephraim will
> be broken to pieces so that it will
> no longer be a people.)
> And the head of Ephraim is Samaria
> and the head of Samaria is the son
> of Remaliah.
>
> כה אמר אדני יהוה לא תקום ולא
> תהיה כי ראש ארם דמשק וראש דמשק
> רצין ובעוד ששים וחמש שנה יחת
> אפרים מעם וראש אפרים שמרון וראש
> שמרון בן רמליהו

(e)   ORDERS

> If you will not believe,
>   surely you shall not be
>   established.
> אם לא תאמינו כי לא
> תאמנו

While this oracle has undoubtedly undergone editorial change and expansion in the course of its transmission, as biblical critics have pointed out,[5] the text as we now have it manifests the conventional language of address to a warrior. There is a Directive using verbs in the imperative. This may seem strange at first since a Directive is characteristic of offensive situations and not the defensive situation in which Ahaz finds himself. However, Yahweh is informing Ahaz that he is really not in a defensive situation and that the appropriate action to take in the face of the enemy is to have confidence in Yahweh, always on the offensive for the king. This becomes clearer in the orders Ahaz is given.

The Assurance is the typical אל תירא and is expanded with the additional phrase ולבבך אל ירך (compare the Assurance in Deut 20:3-4).[6] We noted above that the Assurance is often expanded in offensive situations. Here again the structure of this oracle helps us see that Isaiah's oracle is to comfort Ahaz not in a defensive situation but in the offensive action which the deity has taken against the enemy.

The Object of Fear is introduced by מן as is typical of this element. It is significant that this element in Isa 7 has important parallels in 2 Kgs 19:6//Isa 37:6 suggesting the specific way Isaiah is using this stereotypical language. In both places the Object of Fear is longer than was typical of this element in the Deuteronomic History and in Jeremiah.[7] Also the words of the king of Ephraim and the king of Syria in the Object of Fear in Isa 7 parallel the words of the king of Assyria in the Object of Fear in 2 Kgs 19:6//Isa 37:6.

The introduction of the Basis of Assurance by the prophetic messenger formula, כה אמר אדני יהוה, is not typical of this element. But the formula appears at the beginning of the address in 2 Kgs 19:6//Isa 37:6 and is to be explained by the fact that in both places the words of address to a warrior are spoken by a prophet. The preposition כי, which is typical of this element, does occur but not at the beginning as would be expected. The meaning of the Basis of Assurance is that Ahaz can be assured because the enemy is only human. The enemy has no chance against Yahweh who fights for Ahaz.[8] The Orders are typically constructed in the second person. They are formulated as a condition, as was the case in Jer 42:9-11. This conditional formulation reflects the prophetic adaptation of the genre. There is a significant difference, however, between the conditional Orders given to Ahaz in Isa 7 and the Orders given to the commanders of the forces and the people with them in Jer 42. The Orders in Jer 42 reflect the conditions of the Deuteronomic tradition that promises prosperity and blessing to those who obey the commands of Yahweh and threatens ruin and curse to those who disobey. In Jer 42 failure to obey the conditions of the orders will lead to death by the sword in a foreign land (Jer 42:16). Unlike the Orders given to the larger community in Jer 42, the Orders in Isa 7 are addressed to the king and reflect a different tradition concerning the election of the king. Whereas in the royal traditions in the Hebrew Scriptures, the king will be punished if he does not obey the conditions of the covenant (see Pss 89:31ff.; 132:11-12 and 2 Sam 7:14-16), the promise is that the line of the king will endure.[9] Here again the variation in the use of the genre in these two distinct tradition complexes indicates a difference in the roles of the warriors addressed. In the Deuteronomic complex the community is to take an active role in preserving itself; in the royal complex of traditions it is the deity who takes the active role in preserving the dynasty. In the

Deuteronomic complex the warrior is given orders to be actively engaged in the establishment of security; in the royal complex the king is given orders to trust in the security of knowing that Yahweh is on the offensive to preserve the status quo.

The structure of this oracle addressed to Ahaz, then, follows the stereotypical structure of the genre which we have called the language of address to a warrior in the Deuteronomic History and Jeremiah; but the genre is utilized in a significantly different way when Isaiah employs it to comfort a king faced with a military attack. The king is not given orders to be an active participant in the conflict as is Joshua or Jeremiah; he plays a passive role, and it is the deity who is the warrior who will fight for the king. The conventional and stereotypical language employing the formula, "fear not," is not uniquely associated with one tradition complex in the Hebrew Scriptures. What we want to show in the remaining part of this chapter is that Isaiah's use of the *Gattung* to address a king has parallels in other ancient Near Eastern texts which can be dated roughly during the same time period as Isaiah.[10]

King Zakir of Hamath and Lu'ath

The first text to be considered is part of an historical inscription found on the stela set up by Zakir, king of Hamath and Lu'ath "in connection with the dedication of a statue of Ilu-Wer, an avatar of Hadad."[11] The text is dated in the early years of the eighth century B.C.E.[12] The opening words announce that it was Zakir who set up the stela. After Zakir identifies himself in the first person, he goes on to say how Barhadad, the son of Hazael, king of Aram formed an alliance of kings against him:

> Barhadad, the son of Hazael, king of Aram, united [seven of] a group of ten kings against me: Barhadad and his army; Bargush and his army; the king of Cilicia and his army; the king of 'Umq and his army; the king of Gurgum and his army; the king of Sam'al and his army; the king of Milidh and his army. [All these kings whom Barhadad united against me] were seven kings and their armies. All these kings laid siege to Hatarikka. They made a wall higher than the wall of Hatarikka. They made a moat deeper than its moat.

The situation described here is similar to that of Ahaz in Isa 7 when the kingship of Ahaz was also threatened by a military alliance of enemy kings.

In response to this threat of war created by the military alliance, Zakir says,

> But I lifted up my hand to Beʻelshamayn and Beʻelshamayn heard
> me. Beʻelshamayn [spoke] to me through seers and through *diviners*.

Unlike Ahaz, Zakir seeks the aid of the deity in the face of this military threat to his

kingship. Indeed, the contrast between Zakir and Ahaz highlights Ahaz's refusal to trust

Yahweh—one of the major themes of Isa 7. At any rate Beʻelshamayn does answer the

inquiring Zakir through intermediaries (seers and diviners) with words that are

structurally similar to the language of address to a warrior:

(a)   ASSURANCE

  Do not fear

(b)   BASIS OF ASSURANCE

  for I made you king,

(c)   PROMISE

  and I shall stand by you and deliver you from all [these kings who] set up
  siege against you.

(d)   MESSENGER FORMULA (?)

  [*Beʻelshamayn*] said to me:

(e)   PROMISE

  [*I shall destroy*] all these kings who set up [*a siege against you and made this
  moat*] and this wall which . . .

The Assurance is the expected "Do not fear." There is no Object of Fear, although,

as we will see, this element never occurs in extra-biblical texts and is regularly missing

from the biblical texts that we will investigate below. The Basis of Assurance is

introduced by the word "for" and states the reason for not being afraid, i.e., that

Beʻelshamayn had made Zakir king. While Yahweh's election of the king is not mentioned

in Isa 7, we have argued that Yahweh's election of the king is the implicit reason Ahaz

should have had the confidence to believe he was in no danger and therefore did not need

to intervene militarily. Here the genre does not contain Orders as in Isa 7 but Promises

and in this way is more similar to the oracle Isaiah spoke to Hezekiah (Isa 37:6//2 Kgs

19:6) than to the one he delivered to Ahaz. The Zakir text is damaged so that the

Promise is not complete. When the text resumes, the king is announcing his own great

achievements. In the middle of the Promise the deity is identified as speaking, in what

we have identified as the messenger formula that frequently occurs in the prophetic use

of this genre (see Isa 7:7; 37:6; Jer 1:8; and 42:7). However, it is not strictly a messenger
formula because Zakir is reporting what the deity had communicated to him; it is not the
original communication of the deity through an intermediary that is reported here.

This Zakir text, then, has affinities with what we have termed the language of
address to a warrior, especially as that genre has been employed by the prophet Isaiah.
The setting, like that in Isa 7, is a military alliance that threatens the king. The
structure is similar to that of the genre as we have outlined it in the Hebrew Scriptures.
It contains a Promise like Isaiah's oracle to Hezekiah (Isa 37:6//2 Kgs 19:6) rather than
Orders as in Isa 7:4-9. There is no Object of Fear. These peculiarities in the oracle
addressed to Zakir, as we will see, are matched by the same peculiarities in subsequent
texts that we will discuss in the Hebrew Scriptures: the Object of Fear is missing and a
Promise rather than Orders is part of the structure. The Promise occurs even where
there is a specific military threat and not just in general situations of war as in the
Deuteronomic History (see Deut 20:3-5).

Oracle of Ninlil Concerning Ashurbanipal

This oracle dated in the seventh century B.C.E.[13] follows the same conventional use
of the genre that we have noted in our discussion of the oracles addressed to Ahaz,
Hezekiah and Zakir. The structure of the oracle is:

(a)   ASSURANCE

Fear not,

(b)   ADDRESS

O Ashurbanipal!

(c)   BASIS OF ASSURANCE

Now, as I have spoken, it will come to pass: I shall grant (it) to you. Over
the people of the four languages (and) over *the armament* of the princes you
will exercise sovereignty . . .

(d)   OBJECT OF FEAR

[The kings] of the countries confer together (saying), "Come (let us rise)
against Ashurbanipal . . . The fate of our fathers and our grandfathers (the
Assyrians) have fixed: [let not his might] cause divisions among us."

(e)   PROMISE

[Nin]lil answered saying, "[The kings] of the lands [I shall over]*throw*, place
under the yoke, bind their feet in [strong fetters]. For the second time I
proclaim to you that as with the land of Elam and the Cimmerians [I shall

proceed]. I shall arise, break the thorns, open up widely my way through the *briers*. With *blood* shall I turn the land into a rain shower, (fill it with) lamentation and *wailing*. You ask, 'What lamentation and *wailing*?' Lamentation enters Egypt, *wailing* comes out (from there)."

(f)   CONCLUDING ASSURANCE

Ninlil is his mother. Fear not! The mistress of Arbela bore him. Fear not! As she that bears for *her child*, (so) I care for you. I have placed you like an *amulet* on my breast. At night I place a spread over you, all day I keep a cover on you. In the early morning heed your supplication, heed your conduct. Fear not, my son, whom I have raised.

Here the Assurance is followed by an Address. While the Address has not been a regularly recurring element with "fear not," it has occurred (e.g., Deut 20:3-4) and as we will see is typical of the genre in extra-biblical royal texts[14] and in the Hebrew Scriptures where the community is addressed as king.[15] The Basis of Assurance, which grants Ashurbanipal sovereignty over the people of the four languages and the princes, is similar to those Bases of Assurance in the Hebrew Scriptures which state that the enemy has been given into the hand of the warrior.[16] The Object of Fear does not follow the Assurance as is normally the case. However, it is similar to the Object of Fear in the Isaian oracles to Hezekiah (2 Kgs 19:6//Isa 37:6) and to Ahaz (Isa 7:4-9). As in the Isaian oracles the Object of Fear here quotes the threatening words of the enemy. This oracle, like the oracles to Hezekiah and to Zakir, contains a Promise to the king that the deity will fight for him. There is a concluding Assurance exhorting the king not to fear and containing the motif of the deity's concern for the king from birth. The intervention of the deity in the infancy of the "warrior" has been met before. In Jeremiah the words of assurance to the prophetic warrior are preceded by the deity's declaration that he had known and formed Jeremiah from birth to carry out his vocation. As we will see this motif is picked up in the use of the genre by Second Isaiah to address the community as king (e.g., Isa 44:1-5).[17] Also Second Isaiah's use of the genre sometimes concludes with a final Assurance (e.g., Isa 41:8-13).

The structure of this text, then, reflects the conventions of the genre when it is used to address a king. As in the Isaian oracles the Object of Fear refers to threatening words of the enemy. Also, the oracle does not compel the king to become actively engaged in the battle. Like the oracles addressed to the kings Hezekiah and Zakir, the oracle contains a Promise that the deity will fight for the king against the enemy.

We noted that the oracles addressed to Ahaz, Hezekiah and Zakir were occasioned by a military threat to kingship; so is the Oracle of Ninlil. Furthermore, the setting of this oracle, like that of the oracles to Ahaz and Zakir, is an alliance of enemies threatening the king.

An Oracular Dream Concerning Ashurbanipal

This text, dated in 648 B.C.E.[18] is not as neatly structured as those which we have just considered. Throughout the text, however, are elements of language and conventions associated with what we have called the language of address to a warrior. The text begins as Ashurbanipal recalls how Ishtar had heard his "anxious sighs" and had said to him, "Fear not," which gave him confidence. Similarly King Zakir remembered that Be'elshamayn had heard him and had addressed him with the Assurance, "Do not fear." Again, however, the details of the cultic setting are missing. It is clear, however, that war is associated with the Assurance, "fear not." The deity will fight for the king against an enemy who is mentioned specifically in the text, "Teumman, king of Elam."[19] Ashurbanipal says that during the night a šabrû-priest reclined and saw a dream, and when he awoke he reported the dream to Ashurbanipal as follows:

> The goddess Ishtar who dwells in Arbela came in. Right and left
> quivers were suspended from her. She was holding a bow in her hand,
> and a sharp sword was drawn to do battle. You were standing in
> front of her and she spoke to you like a real mother. Ishtar called to
> you, she who is most exalted among the gods, giving you the
> following instructions: "Wait with the attack; (for) wherever you
> intend to go, I am also ready to go." You said to her, "Wherever you
> go, I will go with you, O goddess of goddesses!" She repeated her
> command to you as follows: "You shall stay here where you should
> be. Eat, drink wine, make merry, praise my divinity, while I go and
> accomplish that work to help you attain your heart's desire. Your
> face will not be pale, nor your feet shaky, and you need not wipe off
> your (cold) sweat in the height of battle." She wrapped you in her
> lovely babysling, protecting your entire body, Her face shone like
> fire. Then [she went out in a frightening way] to defeat your
> enemies, against Teumman, king of Elam, with whom she was angry.

There are several things about this vision that are clearly related to the conventions of war that we have associated with the phrase, "fear not" in the Hebrew Scriptures. We argued above that the Basis of Assurance was sometimes introduced by the imperative of ראה ("see," e.g., Josh 8:1-2 and Deut 1:20-21). The vision itself is a convention of the language of war. We argued that the two visions in Jeremiah's call acted as a Basis of Assurance for the addresses to Jeremiah as a warrior that preceded and followed them. The vision here has the same function, i.e., to further assure Ashurbanipal that he need not fear. Opening with a picture of Ishtar in full battle attire ready for war, this vision is comparable to Elisha's vision of the heavenly army poised for battle (2 Kgs 6:17).[20]

The conversation between the king and the goddess in the vision uses several elements of the conventional language of address to a warrior. Ishtar gives Ashurbanipal a Directive, "Wait for the attack . . ." This Directive in the imperative is like that given to Ahaz in Isa 7:14, "Take heed, be quiet." When Ashurbanipal insists that he is ready to go to war with the goddess, she gives him his Orders, "You shall stay here where you should be," and a further Directive, "Eat, drink wine, make merry, praise my divinity." The Directives and the Orders given to Ashurbanipal are like those Isaiah gives to Ahaz in that the king is not directed or ordered to be actively engaged in the battle. That the king is not to be actively engaged in the battle and that the deity is the one who will do the fighting for him is obvious from the promise she makes to him. She directs him to:

> Eat, drink wine, make merry and praise my divinity, while I go and accomplish that work to help you attain your heart's desire. Your face will not be pale, nor your feet shaky, and you need not wipe off your (cold) sweat in the height of battle.

The non-involvement of the king in the battle against his enemy is also clear from the final reported vision of the deity fighting for the king:

> She wrapped you in her lovely babysling, protecting your entire body. Her face shone like fire. Then [she went out in a frightening way] to defeat your enemies, against Teumman, king of Elam, with whom she was angry.

This oracular dream of Ashurbanipal, then, contains elements associated with "fear not" in the language of address to a warrior. While these elements do not occur in as tightly knit a structure as we have noted in the Hebrew Scriptures (but see 2 Kgs 1:1-16 and 2 Kgs 6:8-23), they do represent elements of the genre and employ the genre as does Isaiah to comfort a king who is not to be an active participant in a forthcoming battle. The king need not fight; the deity will fight for him.

Conclusion

In this chapter we have argued that the prophetic oracle which Isaiah delivers to King Ahaz (Isa 7:4-9) functions similarly to the oracle he delivered to King Hezekiah (2 Kgs 19:6//Isa 37:6). While both oracles follow the conventional language of address to a warrior used in the Deuteronomic History and in Jeremiah, they do not give orders to the king to become actively engaged in battle even though both kings are in defensive military situations. Ahaz is ordered to place his trust in Yahweh, and Hezekiah is promised that the invasion of Sennacherib will come to nought. Kings are not conventional warriors who, like Joshua or the prophetic warrior, Jeremiah, are expected to be actively engaged in battle; they are ordered to play a passive role because it is the deity who will fight for them. It has often been noted that the Deuteronomic History and Jeremiah belong to a different set of traditions than does Isaiah of Jerusalem. Our study further confirms this dichotomy of traditions by arguing that while both sets of traditions employ a common genre, each one employs it in a distinctive fashion. The Deuteronomic tradition (shared by Jeremiah) uses the genre to place emphasis on the active participation in battle by the community and its leader while the royal tradition reflected in Isaiah uses the genre to emphasize the action of the deity on behalf of a community and its leader (the king), who is to take a passive stance of trust in the action of god.

We also examined three extra-biblical texts where a deity addressed a king in defensive military situations.[21] There the use of the language of address to a warrior parallels Isaiah's use of that genre, i.e., the emphasis is placed on the action of the deity who will fight against the enemy of the king while the king is to play a passive role. Interestingly, these two texts represent the same variation in the structure of the genre that we noted in Isaiah's use of it. The significance of this variation will become evident in subsequent chapters. The oracle Isaiah spoke to Hezekiah contained a Promise rather than Orders while the oracle he delivered to Ahaz contained Orders rather than a Promise. Similarly the oracle to Zakir and Ninlil's oracle to Ashurbanipal have a Promise rather than Orders and in Ishtar's oracle to Ashurbanipal he was given Orders rather than a Promise. In the remaining texts which we will examine in the Hebrew Scriptures, this same variation will occur in the structure. The structure will contain either a Promise or Orders.

CHAPTER IV

THE TEMPLE AS CITADEL

Introduction

This chapter will focus on "fear not" texts in the Chronicler's History (including Nehemiah) as well as a "fear not" text in Haggai where the function of the genre is similar. In these late post-exilic texts, the genre is used with its royal connotations, i.e., the emphasis is placed on the action of the deity while the recipient of the oracle takes a more passive stance vis-à-vis the battle. Furthermore, we will see that in these late texts it is the community as a whole and not simply the king whom Yahweh addresses as a warrior for whom he alone will fight. We will also see that while the king and the community are not expected to be active in battle, they are ordered to turn their activity to the construction of the temple in which they direct their praise to Yahweh, a divine warrior who fights for them. The service of these warriors is focused on the temple, which is a citadel of defense against the enemy.

Hezekiah to the Combat Commanders: 2 Chr 32:7-8a

These words are not spoken by the deity to the king but are spoken by the king to his combat commanders. This text reminds us again that the genre is not a typical form of divine speech but is used more generally to address warriors whether the speaker is a deity or a human being. It would therefore be wrong to tie the genre to a specific cultic occasion. The genre is more clearly related to the conventions associated generally with the conduct of war.

The context of Hezekiah's words concerns Sennacherib's invasion of Judah. When Hezekiah learned of the invasion, he took steps to stop up the springs so that Sennacherib's forces would not have water (vss. 2-4). He repaired the wall, built towers on it and made weapons and shields in abundance (vs. 5). He then addressed the combat commanders (שרי מלחמות) whom he had appointed over the people. The words he speaks can be outlined as follows:

(a)   ENCOURAGEMENT

Be strong and of good courage.

חזקו ואמצו

63

(b)   ASSURANCE

        Do not be afraid or dismayed

        אל תיראו ואל תחתו

(c)   OBJECT OF FEAR

        before the king of Assyria and all the horde that is with him;

        מפני מלך אשור ומלפני כל ההמון אשר עמו

(d)   BASIS OF ASSURANCE

        for there is one greater with us than with him. With him is an arm of flesh;
        but with us is the LORD our God,

        כי עמנו רב מעמו עמו זרוע בשר ועמנו יהוה אלהינו

(e)   PROMISE

        to help us and to fight our battles.

        לעזרנו ולהלחם מלחמתנו

These words of Hezekiah follow the conventions that we have identified as characteristic of the language of address to a warrior. Indeed, the structural elements used are an indication of the particular situation. The use of the Object of Fear suggests the defensive situation, i.e., the invasion of Judah by Sennacherib. The Encouragement is typical of situations where warriors have been given a new task to perform as warriors (see above pp. 25-27). Here in preparation for war Hezekiah appointed combat commanders over the people and encouraged them in their new role. The Promise with the infinitive construction is also typical of situations where a warrior or warriors have been appointed to a new task (see above our discussion of Jer. 1:7-8).

The ensuing context makes it clear that in the Chronicler's History, it is the deity and not the people who fight the battle. Sennacherib seeks to create doubt in the people by sending messengers to Jerusalem to question Hezekiah's assurance that Yahweh will deliver the people from the hand of Assyria (vs. 11). He asks the people if the gods of any of the nations have ever delivered a people from Assyria (vss. 13ff.). In vs. 21 it is stated, however, that "Yahweh sent an angel who cut off all the mighty warriors and commanders and officers in the camp of the king of Assyria." Yahweh did fight for his people and gave them the victory so that Sennacherib returned home in shame and was killed by one of his own sons.

In this passage, then, it is the king who addresses warriors and not the king who is addressed as a warrior by the deity. The warriors in this passage, however, conform to the picture of the king as a warrior. They are not ordered to fight; the deity fights for them and gives them the victory.

Yahweh will fight for the Community: 2 Chr 20:15-17

These words are spoken by Jahaziel, a Levite of the sons of Asaph, to the community and to king Jehoshaphat.[1] They show how the genre is extended to include the community and also highlight the importance of the temple as a citadel of defense against the enemy. The following outline indicates that the words spoken by Jahaziel conform to the language of address to a warrior:

(a)   ADDRESS

      Hearken, all Judah and inhabitants of Jerusalem, and King Jehoshaphat:

      הקשיבו כל יהודה וישבי ירושלם והמלך יהושפט

(b)   PROPHETIC MESSENGER FORMULA

      Thus says the LORD to you,

      כה אמר יהוה לכם

(c)   ADDRESS

      you,

      אתם

(d)   ASSURANCE

      fear not, and be not dismayed

      אל תיראו ואל תחתו

(e)   OBJECT OF FEAR

      at this great multitude;

      מפני ההמון הרב הזה

(f)   BASIS OF ASSURANCE

      for the battle is not yours but God's.

      כי לא לכם המלחמה כי לאלהים

(g)   DIRECTIVE

      Tomorrow go down against them;

      מחר רדו עליהם

(h)   ORDERS

behold, they will come up by the ascent of Ziz; you will find them at the end
of the valley, east of the wilderness of Jeruel. You will not need to fight in
this battle;

הנם עלים במעלה הציץ ומצאתם אתם בסוף הנחל פני מדבר ירואל לא לכם
להלחם בזאת

(i)   DIRECTIVE

take your position, stand still, and see the victory of the LORD on your
behalf,

התיצבו עמדו וראו את ישועת יהוה עמכם

(j)   ADDRESS

O Judah and Jerusalem.

יהודה וירושלם

(k)   ASSURANCE

Fear not, and be not dismayed;

אל תיראו ואל תחתו

(l)   DIRECTIVE

tomorrow go out against them,

מחר צאו לפניהם

(M)   BASIS OF ASSURANCE

And the LORD will be with you.

ויהוה עמכם

The structure of the core of the text (elements d through i) with Assurance, Object
of Fear, Basis of Assurance, two Directives and Orders is virtually identical with the
pattern of the genre as we outlined it in the Deuteronomic History and in Jeremiah,
especially when the genre is used in offensive situations. Furthermore, the elements
display the same characteristics.   The Assurance is the expected אל תיראו, here
expanded with the additional phrase אל תחתו (a feature also characteristic of offensive
situations, cf. Josh 8:1-2). The Object of Fear is introduced by מפני, and the Basis of
Assurance by כי. The Directives are in the imperative, and the Orders are formulated in
the second person.

However, the text manifests the peculiarities that we have associated with the use
of the genre when a king is addressed. Although the Directives suggest an address to a
warrior before an offensive battle, the use of the Object of Fear is characteristic of
defensive and not offensive situations. We noticed this same combination of elements in
our discussion of Isaiah's oracle addressed to King Ahaz in Isa 7:4-9 where the Object of
Fear, characteristic of defensive situations, was used in conjunction with a Directive,

characteristic of offensive situations. We argued that while Ahaz was in a defensive situation, the deity was on the offensive fighting for the king. Similarly, here, while the community is in a defensive situation, the deity is on the offensive fighting for the people. Furthermore, the Directives here are similar to the Directive in Isa 7:4-9. In the Deuteronomic History and in Jeremiah, the Directives were used to give a command to initiate an offensive battle against the enemy. When a king is given Directives, they instruct him to be inactive. The Directive here, "take your position, stand still, and see the victory of the LORD on your behalf," is similar in intent to the Directive Isaiah gives to Ahaz, "Take heed, be quiet."

The text contains three Addresses. The third Address where the community is mentioned by name, "O Judah and Jerusalem," is characteristic of the genre as it is used in texts which we have yet to examine. The first Address, which is a summons to hear, "Hearken (הקשיבו) all Judah and inhabitants of Jerusalem, and king Jehoshaphat," and the second Address which is the pronoun, אתם , are very similar to the Address in Deut 20:3, "Hear (שמע), O Israel, you (אתם)." As we will see, this summons to hear and the personal form of address using the second person is important in Second Isaiah's use of the genre to address the community as king. We will also make the point below that, when this genre is used to address the community, some of the elements will recur at the end of the unit. This is especially true of the Assurance and the Basis of Assurance which recur here along with an Address and a Directive. In short, then, the stereotypical language used here to address the community as warriors is the same as that used in the Deutreronomic History to address warriors. However, here the genre has the peculiarities that we have associated with it when it is used to address a king.

The *Sitz im Text* of the genre in 2 Chr 20 also shows that it is used in a generally military situation and specifically in a military situation which represents a threat to kingship. Chapter 20 begins by mentioning how a coalition of nations created a military threat to the king, Jehoshaphat:

> After this the Moabites and Ammonites and with them some of the Meunites, came against Jehoshaphat for battle.

—2 Chr 20:1

The coalition is reminiscent of those military alliances that threatened the kingship of Ahaz (Isa 7), Zakir, and Ashurbanipal.[2] When Jehoshaphat heard of this coalition, "he

feared" (ויּרא) and "set himself to seek the LORD, and proclaimed a fast throughout all
Judah" (vs. 3). Here Jehoshaphat, unlike Ahaz, but like Zakir and Ashurbanipal, seeks
divine guidance in this time of military threat to his kingship. However, not just the king
but the community as well seeks divine guidance, as is evident in vs. 4 where we are told
the community of Judah along with the king assembled in Jerusalem to seek the LORD.
Jehoshaphat's prayer on behalf of the community (vss. 5-12) asks for divine aid to counter
the military threat under which the community is powerless to defend itself (vs. 12). In
response to this prayer the community is addressed as a warrior and given orders not to
fight.

After Yahweh's address to the community (20:15-17) through Jahaziel, Jehoshaphat
gives further instructions to the community before the battle (vs. 20). He summons the
community to hear in a way that resembles Yahweh's earlier summons to the community
(vs. 15),

> Hear me, Judah and inhabitants of Jerusalem.
> שמעוני יהודה וישבי ירושלם

> —2 Chr 20:20

He then gives them the following Directive:

> Believe in the LORD your God, and you will be established;
> believe his prophets, and you will succeed.
> האמינו ביהוה אלהיכם ותאמנו האמינו בנביאיו והצליחו

> —2 Chr 20:20

This Directive is strikingly similar—only stated positively rather than negatively—to the
Orders Yahweh gives to Ahaz through the prophet Isaiah in Isa 7:9:

> If you will not believe,
> surely you shall not be established.
> אם לא תאמינו כי לא תאמנו

Indeed, Jehoshaphat's added warning to believe in the prophets may be a lesson drawn
from the occasion in which King Ahaz refused to believe in Isaiah the prophet. The
community is not ordered or directed to participate in the battle, but to believe in
Yahweh and his prophets.

The ensuing context makes it clear that the community is to sing praise to Yahweh
(vss. 20-21a) who fights for the community by seeing to it that the enemy armies destroy
one another (vs. 22bff.). Again we have a parallel with the Ashurbanipal text in which he
was directed to praise Ishtar while the goddess fought for him.[3] After the battle in

which the community does not fight, the community takes the spoils of war and returns to the "house of the LORD" (vs. 28). As the concluding verses make clear, the house of the LORD is the source of confidence for the community.

> They came to Jerusalem, with harps and lyres and trumpets, to the house of the LORD. And the fear of God came on all the kingdoms of the countries when they heard that the LORD had fought against the enemies of Israel. So the realm of Jehoshaphat was quiet, for his God gave him rest round about.
>
> —2 Chr 20:28-30

This notion of the temple as a kind of citadel against the enemy is evident from the prayer of Jehoshaphat in vss. 5-12. Jehoshaphat stands in the house of the LORD and prays to Yahweh whom he identifies as God in heaven who rules over kingdoms and nations. He states that Yahweh had driven the inhabitants out of the land which he gave to the people of Israel, who built a sanctuary for Yahweh. When the people come to the house of Yahweh and cry to him, Yahweh will hear the people and save them from the evil which comes upon them. The temple, then, is a refuge, in this instance against the military threat of the military alliance of the Ammonites, the Moabites and the Meunites. In the prayer, Jehoshaphat identifies the community as "the descendants of Abraham your (i.e., Yahweh's) friend" (אברהם אהבך), in vs. 7.[4] This motif of the community as descendants of the patriarch Abraham will emerge again in our examination of those "fear not" texts in which the community is addressed as warriors who, like the king, do not have battles to fight.

It will help before going on to other passages to summarize the discussion of 2 Chr 20. In this chapter the community is addressed with stereotypical language associated with warriors. Furthermore, the community is addressed as are kings, not ordered to fight but to patiently wait and believe in the deity who will fight the battle. This chapter identifies two other motifs: the community as the descendants of Abraham and the importance of the temple as the citadel against the enemy. In subsequent chapters the importance of the patriarchs, most notably Abraham, in connection with this genre when it is used to address the community will be stressed. The remaining part of this chapter will deal with the genre as it is used in connection with the temple as a citadel.

David Addresses Solomon in His Task of Building the Temple: 1 Chr 22:13 and 28:20

In these two passages David gives comfort to Solomon in his vocation as the king who is given the task of building the temple. In both passages he uses the language of address to a warrior. In neither case, however, is Solomon given orders to fight in a battle. His task is to build the temple which becomes a citadel against the enemy, assuring peace for Israel.

In 1 Chr 22 David announces his preparations for the construction of the temple and indicates that Solomon is to carry out the actual building of the temple. David explains to Solomon that he had wanted to build a house for Yahweh but that the word of Yahweh came to him and said,

> You have shed much blood and have waged great wars (ומלחמות
> גדלות עשית); you shall not build a house to my name because you
> have shed so much blood before me upon the earth.
>
> —1 Chr 22:8

David is not given permission to build the temple because he has been a warrior in a conventional sense. Solomon will be a different kind of king, as Yahweh indicates to David:

> Behold, a son shall be born to you; he shall be a man of peace
> (מנוחה). I will give him peace from all his enemies round about; for
> his name shall be Solomon, and I will give peace (שלום) and quiet to
> Israel in his days.
>
> —2 Chr 22:9

Solomon will be a king who will not need to fight; Yahweh will insure him peace against his enemies and will guarantee that his throne will be established forever (vs. 10). He is not to be an active warrior but is to put his trust in Yahweh.

It is significant that David addresses Solomon later on in the chapter with elements that come from the language of address to a warrior. After assuring Solomon that Yahweh would be with him and exhorting him to use understanding and discretion and to obey the law of the LORD, David addresses Solomon with two elements of the language of address to a warrior (vs. 13):

(a)   ENCOURAGEMENT

Be strong and of good courage.

(b)   ASSURANCE

Fear not; and be not dismayed.
אל תירא ואל תחת

Here the Encouragement is used because Solomon is being assigned a new task. The assurance is given to Solomon as a king whose deity will fight his enemies and give him peace.

Later in 1 Chr 28 David transmits the final plans for building the temple to Solomon and speaks to Solomon by employing in a more developed form the language of address to the king as warrior. The chapter opens by indicating that David assembled all the officials of Jerusalem including the "mighty men" (הגבורים) and "all the seasoned warriors" (כל גבור חיל). When he addresses this assembly he reiterates what he had said to Solomon in chapter 22, i.e., that he had intended to build a house for Yahweh and that Yahweh had refused saying,

You may not build a house for my name, for you are a
warrior (איש מלחמות) and you have shed blood.

—1 Chr 28:3

He goes on to say that Yahweh had chosen Solomon to build his house and that Yahweh would establish Solomon's kingdom for ever (vss. 6-7). He exhorts Solomon to be obedient to Yahweh. After giving Solomon the final plans for the temple (vss. 11-19), he addresses Solomon as a king who has no wars to fight. David's words to Solomon (vs. 20-21) can be outlined as follows.

(a)   ENCOURAGEMENT

Be strong and of good courage,
חזק ואמץ

(b)   DIRECTIVE

and do it.
ועשה

(c)   ASSURANCE

Fear not, be not dismayed;
אל תירא ואל תחת

(d)   BASIS OF ASSURANCE

for the LORD God, even my God, is with you
כי יהוה אלהים אלהי עמך

(e)   PROMISE

He will fail you or forsake you, until all the work for the service of the
house of the LORD is finished. And behold the divisions of the priests and
the Levites for all the service of the house of God; and with you in all the
work will be every willing man who has skill for any kind of service; also the
officers and all the people will be wholly at your command.
לא ירפך ולא יעזבך עד לכלות כל מלאכת עבודת בית יהוה והנה מחלקות
הכהנים והלוים לכל עבודת בית האלהים ועמך בכל מלאכה לכל נדיב בחכמה
לכל עבודה והשרים וכל העם לכל דבריך

Here the Encouragement is used to exhort Solomon to fulfill a new vocation as the

builder of the temple. It is formulated with the typical phrase, חזק ואמץ. The Directive

is in the imperative and the Assurance is the typical אל תירא with the accompanying

phrase ואל ותחת which often occurs in an Assurance.   The Basis of Assurance is

introduced with כי and assures Yahweh's presence with Solomon. Here the Basis of

Assurance and the Promise are formulated in the third person because David is speaking

about Yahweh. When Yahweh is the speaker, these two elements are formulated in the

first person.

These two texts utilize the language of address to the king as warrior. David uses

this genre to address Solomon who is given the vocation to build the temple as a citadel

against the enemy. Here the genre has parallels to its use when a king is addressed as a

warrior; Solomon will not be a conventional warrior who himself sheds blood and fights

battles. Indeed, because David was just such a conventional warrior, Yahweh forbade

him to build the temple. The temple, the house of Yahweh, is the defense against the

enemy. It is therefore not necessary for Solomon to be a warrior in the conventional

sense.

The Rebuilding of the Temple in the Post-Exilic Period: Hag 2:4-9

In this passage Haggai uses the language of address to a warrior to comfort

Zerubbabel, the governor of Judah, Joshua, the high priest and all the remnant of the

people. The situation concerns the rebuilding of the temple in the post-exilic period.

The genre functions in this passage concerning the rebuilding of the temple similarly to

the way it functioned in the passage in which David comforted Solomon who initially built the temple. The structure of Haggai's words can be outlined as follows:

(a) INTRODUCTION

Yet now
ועתה

(b) ENCOURAGEMENT

take courage,
חזק

(c) ADDRESS

O Zerubbabel,
זרבבל

(d) PROPHETIC FORMULA

says the LORD;
נאם יהוה

(e) ENCOURAGEMENT

take courage,
וחזק

(f) ADDRESS

O Joshua, son of Jehozadak, the high priest;
יהושע בן יהוצדק הכהן הגדול

(g) ENCOURAGEMENT

take courage,
וחזק

(h) ADDRESS

all you people of the land,
כל עם הארץ

(i) PROPHETIC FORMULA

says the LORD;
נאם יהוה

(j) DIRECTIVE

work,
ועשו

(k)   BASIS OF ASSURANCE

for I am with you, says the LORD of hosts, according to the promise that I made you when you came out of Egypt. My spirit abides among you;

כי אני אתכם נאם יהוה צבאות את הדבר אשר כרתי אתכם בצאתכם ממצרים ורוחי עמדת בתוככם

(l)   ASSURANCE

fear not.

אל תיראו

(m)   PROMISE

For thus says the LORD of hosts: Once again, in a little while, I will shake the heavens and the earth and the sea and the dry land; and I will shake all nations, so that the treasures of all the nations shall come in, and I will fill this house with splendor, says the LORD of hosts. The silver is mine, and the gold is mine, says the LORD of hosts. The latter splendor of this house shall be greater than the former, says the LORD of hosts; and in this place I will give prosperity, says the LORD of hosts.

כי כה אמר יהוה צבאות עוד אחת מעט היא ואני מרעיש את השמים ואת הארץ ואת הים ואת החרבה והרעשתי את כל הגוים ובאו חמדת כל הגוים ומלאתי את הבית הזה כבוד אמר יהוה צבאות לי הכסף ולי הזהב נאם יהוה צבאות גדול יהיה כבוד הבית הזה האחרון מן הראשון אמר יהוה צבאות ובמקום הזה אתן שלום נאם יהוה צבאות

These words of Haggai follow the convention of the language of address to a warrior and are strikingly similar to the words David spoke to Solomon (1 Chr 28:20) before he built the temple. The introductory ועתה sets up a contrast with the question raised in vs. 3 concerning the abysmal state of the present temple site. It is not a typical element in the genre as we have outlined it.[5] Since Zerubbabel, Joshua and the remnant of the people are being appointed to a new task of building the temple, the Encouragement חזק is used and parallels the Encouragement given to Solomon in 1 Chr 22:13 and 28:20. The Directive ועשו also parallels the Directive given to Solomon in 1 Chr 28:20. The remaining elements are typical of the genre. The Addresses used here reflect the convention of addressing a king by name. The Basis of Assurance is introduced by כי and emphasizes the presence of Yahweh with the warriors, a motif characteristic of this element. The Assurance is the expected אל תיראו . In the Promise Yahweh promises in the first person that he will restore the temple to a splendor that will far surpass even the splendor of the original temple.

One question needs to be raised in our discussion of Hag 2:4-9: "Why would Haggai use the language of address to a warrior to comfort those who are to rebuild the temple of Yahweh?" It is our contention that the genre functions here in the same way as it functions in the book of Chronicles. It is used to comfort those who are given the responsibility to build the temple as a citadel against the enemy. Yahweh, whose presence is guaranteed by the temple, will fight the battle against the enemy. Indeed, in the Promise Yahweh promises that he will fight for his people and fill the temple with riches gathered from the nations. It is in the context of Yahweh fighting as a cosmic warrior that we are to understand the following words of Yahweh announced in the Promise,

> I will shake the heavens and the earth (ואני מרעיש את השמים ואת הארץ) and the sea and dry land; and I will shake all nations (והרעשתי את כל הגוים), so that the treasures of all nations shall come in, and I will fill this house with splendor, says the LORD of hosts.

These words are very similar to the words Haggai is ordered to speak to Zerubbabel assuring him of the establishment of the kingdom (Hag 2:21-22).

> Speak to Zerubbabel, governor of Judah, saying, I am about to shake the heavens and the earth (אני מרעיש את השמים ואת הארץ), and to overthrow the throne of kingdoms; I am about to destroy the strength of the kingdoms of the nations, and overthrow the chariots and their riders; and the horses and their riders shall go down, every one by the sword of his fellow.

Here the military intentions of Yahweh's cosmic war against the nations are quite explicit. By shaking the heavens and the earth Yahweh will fight for Zerubbabel and assure his reign as Messiah (see Hag 2:23). The context of Hag 2, then, makes it clear that we are dealing with a tradition in which Yahweh will fight for the king and give him the victory. Here the warring activity is extended to include the high priest, Joshua, and all the remnant of the people. Here, as in the book of Chronicles, the temple has become a citadel against the enemy. In the context of this chapter, the use of the language of address to a warrior makes good sense; it is used to address Zerubbabel, Joshua and the people of the land, who, like a king, have no battles to fight. They are comforted knowing that the deity will fight on their behalf.

Nehemiah Comforts the Community: Neh 4:8

This text in Nehemiah needs to be considered in our discussion of "fear not" texts associated with the Chronicler's History. The context of the passage concerns the threat of Sanballat and his associates who came to fight against Jerusalem when they

discovered that the walls of Jerusalem were rebuilt (Neh 4:1-3; Eng. 4:7-9). In response
to this threat Nehemiah stationed the people who were armed with swords, spears and
bows (Neh 4:7; Eng. 4:13). The words Nehemiah uses to address the people in this
defensive situation can be outlined as follows:

(a)   ASSURANCE

Do not be afraid
אל תיראו

(b)   OBJECT OF FEAR

of them.
מפניהם

(c)   DIRECTIVE

Remember the Lord, who is great and terrible, and fight for your brethren,
your sons, your daughters, your wives and your homes.
את אדני הגדול והנורא זכרו והלחמו על אחיכם בניכם ובנתיכם נשיכם ובתיכם

These words of Nehemiah contain an Assurance, an Object of Fear and a Directive.
Furthermore, these elements are constructed in a characteristic way. The Assurance is
the typical אל תיראו, the Object of Fear is introduced by מפני and the Directive is in the
imperative. There is an anomaly, however, in this combination of elements. The use of
the Object of Fear would indicate a defensive situation while the Directive would
indicate an offensive situation. We noted in our discussion of the genre when it was used
to address a king that the Object of Fear is sometimes used with a Directive or
Directives (for example, see above the discussion of Isa 7:4-9). However, when a king is
given a Directive, it is to be still. Here the Directive is to fight. Indeed, this text is
unlike the other texts we have considered in this chapter in that the community here is
directed to be actively engaged in the fighting against the enemy. The warriors here
follow more closely the Joshua paradigm than the paradigm of the king as warrior.

There are other peculiarities in the structure of this text. There is no Basis of
Assurance although the first part of the Directive, which exhorts the people to remember
the LORD, acts as a kind of Basis of Assurance. Also, there are no Orders given even
though the Directive is for the people to actively fight the enemy.

The peculiar situation here may explain the formulation of the words spoken by
Nehemiah. There are no Orders given because the situation does not concern a specific
battle. Instead, there is a Directive instructing the people to be prepared to fight if such
a situation should eventuate. There is a kind of initiative required by the people if they

are to defend themselves. The Object of Fear is used because there is a threat from the enemy. The situation is not one of outright attack but of a state of preparedness against the enemy.

Our understanding of the conventions of war also may give us some insight into the opening words of Neh 4:8, which preface Nehemiah's address to the community. He says,

> And I looked (וארא) and arose (ואקום), and said to the nobles of the
> rest of the people . . .

Some commentators have had trouble understanding the opening words, "and I looked," as is evident from the note in BHS which suggests that a phrase such as כי יראו, should be inserted. There is no textual evidence for such an insertion. However, it is our contention that this phraseology makes sense given the conventions of the language of war. We noted above that there is no Basis of Assurance in Neh 4:8 and that even though it is a defensive situation, the form follows what is expected in an offensive situation. It will be recalled from our discussion of the genre in the Deuteronomic History that in offensive situations the Basis of Assurance was often introduced by the imperative ראה (see Josh 8:1-2). Indeed, in our discussion of Jer 1 we saw the importance of seeing (ראה) as strengthening the Assurance. Also, it will be recalled that in offensive situations the Directive often contained the imperative "arise" (קום); see for example, Josh 8:1-2. It is possible to conjecture here that Nehemiah's words, "I looked" and "I arose" are in response to a previous address of Yahweh to him concerning the possible attack of the enemy. If that is the case, then the Directive he gives the people is a relay of the Directive Yahweh had given to him (cf. Deut 1:19ff.). At any rate vs. 15 indicates divine intervention when it says that the enemy heard that God had frustrated their plan.

Neh 4, then, is a unique text in the Chronicler's History. It is a text addressed to warriors who are to be actively engaged in the battle. Although Yahweh will fight for the people (see Neh 4:14), the people are not directed to inactivity.

Conclusion

The following concluding observations can be made about the use of the language of address to a warrior in the Chronicler's History and in Haggai. In Nehemiah the genre is used to address warriors who, like Joshua, are ordered and directed to be engaged in a battle against the enemy. The other texts use the genre to address warriors who, like a king, are directed and ordered *not* to fight battles because it is the deity who will fight for the warrior. In these texts, however, the use of the genre to address the king has been extended to include the community. Like kings, the community is not ordered or directed to be engaged in war. Furthermore, these texts highlight the importance of the temple as a citadel against the enemy. The king and community do not fight wars; the activity of these non-conventional warriors is directed towards building the temple. It is in singing and praising Yahweh in the temple that one serves Yahweh, not in fighting alongside Yahweh in battles. Indeed, because David was a conventional warrior, he was ordered by Yahweh not to carry out the building of the temple. That task was left to Solomon who would be a different sort of king—a king who would be a man of peace (1 Chr 22:9). When Haggai encouraged the returned exiles to rebuild the temple, he also saw that Yahweh would fight for the peoples against the nations, establishing peace for the post-exilic community and granting the people the riches gathered from the defeated nations. We also noted in our discussion of 2 Chr 20 that the community for which Yahweh fights is identified as the offspring of Abraham, Yahweh's friend. In the next two chapters we will examine other "fear not" texts in which the importance of the patriarchs, especially Abraham, as ancestors of the community for whom Yahweh fights in order to establish peace, is stressed.

CHAPTER V

THE COMMUNITY AS KING IN SECOND ISAIAH

Introduction

Our analysis of "fear not" texts in Second Isaiah will focus on Isa 41:8-16; 43:1-7; and 44:1-5. These three texts comprise five units (41:8-13; 41:14-16; 43:1-4; 43:5-7) which form critics have usually understood as Oracles of Salvation.[1] It is our contention, however, that these texts conform to what we have called the language of address to a warrior[2] and that, while the genre is employed exclusively in Second Isaiah to address the community, it is used in a way which parallels its use to address a king.[3] The royal connotations are evident in the structure of the genre as it is employed by Second Isaiah. We noted above[4] that when a king is comforted before a battle, the genre may contain either Orders or a promise. The two units in 41:8-16 contain Orders while the three units in 43:1-7 and 44:1-5 contain Promises. This variation in the structure of the genre is similar to that employed by Isaiah to address King Ahaz (Isa 7:4-9) and King Hezekiah (Isa 37:6//2 Kgs 19:6); Ahaz was given Orders while Hezekiah was given a Promise. Furthermore, the genre has functional resemblances to the genre in royal contexts. Kings are not ordered to become actively engaged in battle, as were Joshua and other military leaders in the Deuteronomic tradition, but are to take a more detached stance vis-à-vis the actual fighting. Such a detached stance characterizes the role of the community (Jacob/Israel) in Second Isaiah.

Second Isaiah's use of the genre also has parallels in the Chronicler's History and in Haggai. The vocation of the community in Second Isaiah—to celebrate and witness to the victory of Yahweh—is similar to the role of the community in the Chronicler's History and in Haggai; to praise Yahweh in the temple. Second Isaiah, however, does not associate the celebration specifically with the temple but with the victory march to Zion/Jerusalem. It our discussion of 2 Chr 20 we noted that the community for whom Yahweh would fight to establish peace was associated with Abraham, Yahweh's friend. In Second Isaiah the patriarch, Abraham, is the paradigmatic figure representing the community for whom Yahweh is fighting to establish peace.

War Oracles Addressed to a King: The Structure of Isa 41:8-16

In Isa 41:8-16 there are two units (41:8-13 and 41:14-16) each of which follows the conventional language of address to a warrior. The structure of these units can be outlined as follows:

Isa 41:8-13

(a)   ADDRESS

But you, Israel, my servant,
  Jacob, whom I have chosen,
  the offspring of Abraham, my friend;
you whom I took from the ends of the earth,
  and called from its farthest corners,
  saying to you, "You are my servant,
  I have chosen you and not cast you off;"

ואתה ישראל עבדי יעקב אשר בחרתיך
זרע אברהם אהבי
אשר החזקתיך מקצות הארץ ומאצליה קראתיך
ואמר לך עבדי אתה בחרתיך ולא מאסתיך

(b)   ASSURANCE

fear not//be not dismayed,
אל תירא//אל תשתע

(c)   BASIS OF ASSURANCE

for I am with you//I am your God;
I have strengthened you, I have helped you,
  I have upheld you with my victorious right hand.[5]

כי עמך אני//כי אני אלהיך
אמצתיך אף עזרתיך אף תמכתיך בימין צדקי

(d)   ORDERS

Behold, all who are incensed against you
  shall be put to shame and confounded;
those who strive against you
  shall be as nothing and shall perish.
You shall seek those who contend with you,
  but you shall not find them;
those who war against you
  shall be as nothing at all.

הן יבשו ויכלמו כל הנחרים בך
יהיו כאין ויאבדו אנשי ריבך
תבקשם ולא המצאם אנשי מצתך
יהיו כאין וכאפס אנשי מלחמתך

(e)   BASIS OF ASSURANCE

For I, the LORD your God,
  hold your right hand;
it is I who say to you, "Fear not, I will help you."

כי אני יהוה אלהיך מחזיק ימינך
האמר לך אל תירא אני עזרתיך

Isa 41:14-16

(a) ASSURANCE

Fear not,
אל תיראי

(b) ADDRESS

you worm Jacob, you men of Israel!
תולעת יעקב מתי ישראל

(c) BASIS OF ASSURANCE

I have helped you, says the LORD;
    your redeemer is the holy one of Israel.
Behold, I have made you a threshing sledge,
    new, sharp and having teeth;[5]
אני עזרתיך נאם יהוה וגאלך קדוש ישראל
הנה שמתיך למורג חרוץ חדש בעל פיפיות

(d) ORDERS

You shall thresh the mountains and crush them,
    and you shall make the hills like chaff;
you shall winnow them and the wind shall carry them away,
    and the tempest shall scatter them.
And you shall rejoice in the LORD;
    in the Holy One of Israel you shall glory.
תדוש הרים ותדק וגבעות כמץ תשים
תזרם ורוח תשאם וסערה תפיץ אותם
ואתה תגיל ביהוה בקדוש ישראל תתהלל

The structure of each of these two units conforms to the conventions of what we have called the language of address to a warrior. The Assurance is the expected אל תירא. In 41:8-13 it is expanded with the parallel phrase אל תשתע; an additional phrase often occurs in the Assurance in other places where the genre is used. In 41:14-16 the Assurance is in the feminine, אל תיראי , because the community is addressed as a worm (תולעת) which is feminine. In 41:8-13 the Basis of Assurance is introduced by כי and, characteristically, verbs in the perfect tense and in the first person are used. Also typical of this element is the motif of Yahweh's presence with (עם) the warrior. Although כי is missing in the Basis of Assurance in 41:14-16, the verbs are in the perfect tense. The orders are formulated in the second person singular in both texts.

Several characteristics of the structure of the genre as it is employed by Second Isaiah are consistent with address to a king. That the Orders do not compel Israel to be actively engaged in fighting is typical of the genre when it is used to assure a king. There is no Object of Fear, an element that is sometimes missing when a king is addressed.[6] (Of course, the missing Object of Fear matches the content here, as we shall

see, because there are no enemies for the community to fight.) The recurrence of the
Basis of Assurance has been seen, especially in royal contexts.[7] In both units there is an
Address which sometimes occurs when the genre is used in a regal setting (See 2 Chr
20:15-17).[8]

War Oracles Addressed to a King in Isa 41:8-16 and the Literary Context

These two pericopes use the stereotypical language of address to a warrior. That
the genre follows the structural conventions associated with a royal setting, we argue,
heightens the appropriateness of the pericopes to the literary context in which Israel's
role in battle is depicted as the non-combatant role of a king. In short, the genre is not
here by chance as part of a collection of unrelated units of speech but makes sense in its
present *Sitz im Text*.

A clue to the textual setting of the genre is found in the phrase "but you" (ואתה)
which opens the first unit. We have noted before that the second person pronoun
sometimes occurs in an Address.[9] In this instance the phrase, ואתה, introduces a contrast
between the community addressed in 41:8-16 and the nations described in the
immediately preceding verses 41:5-7. Whereas Yahweh assures the community
Jacob/Israel with the comforting "fear not" in 41:10, 13 and 14 and gives the community
orders in 41:11-12 and 15b-16, the nations described in the earlier verses have not
received an assuring "fear not;" they are afraid:

> The coastlands have seen and are afraid (ויראו)
> the ends of the earth tremble (יחרדו).

> —Isa 41:5ab

Nor have they received orders from the deity; instead they are busy making their own
gods and encouraging one another.

> Every one helps his neighbour,
>   and says to his brother, "Take courage (חזק)!"
> The craftsman encourages (ויחזק) the goldsmith,
>   and he who smooths with the hammer him who strikes the anvil,
> saying of the soldering, "It is good;"
>   and they fasten it with nails so that it cannot be moved.

> —Isa 41:6-7

We have noted above that a warrior preparing for battle is frequently encouraged with
the imperative (חזק). For example, Yahweh used this word to encourage Joshua whom he

appointed to lead Israel in battle.[10]   This word of encouragement (חזק) was also
associated with orders or exhortation to build the temple as a defense against the enemy,
as in the address to Solomon in 1 Chr 22:13 and 28:20 and the encouragement of
Zerubbabel, Joshua and the remnant of the people in Hag 2:3-9. The motif of the
building of temple as a citadel is also implied in the pericope in which the nations are
making gods as a defense; making gods is associated with building or refurbishing a
temple.

But what have the nations seen (ראו), [11] and what are they afraid of? They have
seen the victorious and relentless conqueror described in the preceding court scene,
41:1-4. They have no one to reassure them because they do not know what Israel knows:
that it is Yahweh who has done this (41:4), that it is Yahweh "who stirred up one from the
east whom victory (צדק) meets at every step" (41:2). It is Yahweh who comforts Israel in
the Basis of Assurance with the words, "I have upheld you with my victorious (צדקי) right
hand" (41:10). While the nations encourage one another in the desperate attempt to make
idols (41:6-7), Israel is comforted by Yahweh who is in control of things. But the contrast
can be extended even further. This idol passage (41:6-7) needs to be read in conjunction
with the even earlier idol passage (40:18-20). When Yahweh addresses Jacob/Israel as a
warrior in 41:8-16, Israel/Jacob is reminded that Yahweh has chosen him, "But you, Israel
my servant, Jacob, whom I have chosen" (בחרתיך). That is in striking contrast to the
description of idol makers who are not chosen but who themselves must choose good
wood to make their god.

> The idol! a workman casts it,
> and a goldsmith overlays it with gold,
> and casts for it silver chains.
> He who is impoverished chooses (יבחר) for an offering
> wood that will not rot;
> he seeks out a skilled craftsman
> to set up an image that will not move.
>
> —Isa 40:19-20

This idea that the nations, unlike Israel, choose their gods is also evident in 41:24 where
Yahweh says of the gods,

> Behold, you are nothing,
> and your work is nought;
> an abomination is he who chooses you (יבחר בכם).

It will be helpful now to review the way the language of address to the community as a warrior in 41:8-16 relates to the preceding context. Isa 41 opens with a trial scene where the nations are asked to testify to the source of the power behind the conqueror (Cyrus). It is in this unit that war imagery is introduced. The nations are not able to answer because they do not know what Israel knows: that Yahweh is responsible for giving victory to the warrior Cyrus. The scene shifts in vss. 5-7 to the nations who are building idols. They do not know who is responsible for giving victory to the new conqueror, but in fear and trembling they encourage one another to build idols as a defense against the enemy. In sharp contrast to the frantic activity of the nations is Israel's role. Addressed in 41:8-16 as a warrior king by Yahweh, who as we know fights for his king, the community is not even to be actively engaged in fighting in the forthcoming battle.

We will look shortly at the orders Yahweh gives to the regal community. However, a few more words need to be said about the preceding material. Before the trial scene in 41:1-4, there is a disputation in which Yahweh questions Jacob/Israel (40:27-31). We contend that these disputation questions are paralleled in Mesopotamian texts in which the deity addresses kings, especially Esarhaddon, as warriors.[12]   Yahweh asks Jacob/Israel;

> Why do you say, O Jacob,
>   and speak, O Israel,
> "My way is hid from the LORD,
>   and my right is disregarded by my God?"
> Have you not known? Have you not heard?

—Isa 40:27-28b

These questions are comparable to the disputation questions in extra-biblical texts employing the language of address to the king as warrior, for example, the disputation question in what we have called Oracle #1 addressed to Esarhaddon,

> What order have I given you which you did not rely upon?[13]

or in Oracle #3 also addressed to Esarhaddon,

> Where is there any enemy who *overcame* you while I remained
> quiet?[14]

The use of these disputation questions, then, is another indication that Second Isaiah, in addressing the community as warrior, is following conventions associated with the use of the genre when it is utilized to address a king as warrior. The disputation questions function as a means of persuasion.[15] Indeed, all the material preceding the warrior language in 41:8-16 seems to be designed to persuade Israel that Yahweh's words to the community can be believed. The poem concerning the incomparability of Yahweh as creator (40:12-26), the disputation questions to the community (40:27-31), the scene of the trial in which the nations have no testimony (41:1-4), and the frantic and fruitless activity of the nations (41:5-7)—all argue for the credibility of Yahweh's address to the community as warrior-king. The element of persuasion is also to be found in Isaiah's attempt to persuade Ahaz by challenging Ahaz to ask for a sign (Isa 7:11).

The Role of Israel as Warrior-King

Before moving on to consider the material which follows this language of address to Jacob/Israel as a warrior (41:17-29) it will be necessary to consider aspects of the content of the two units themselves (41:8-13 and 41:14-16).

Why would Second Isaiah use the language of address to a warrior? It would seem on the surface to be inappropriate because we are told in the opening of the book that Israel's warfare is ended.

> Comfort, comfort my people,
>   says your God.
> Speak tenderly to Jerusalem,
>   and cry to her
> that her warfare (צְבָאָהּ) is ended,
>   that her iniquity is pardoned,
> that she has received from the LORD's hand
>   double for all her sins.

—Isa 40:1-2

Yet Isaiah employs the language of address to a warrior again in 41: 8-16, in those parts of the oracles which we have called the Orders, to offer the same words of comfort with which the book opens, i.e., to announce to Israel that her warfare has ended. The language of address to a warrior is appropriate only because Israel is like a king; and the king's role is a passive one, as Yahweh fights on his behalf. When a warrior following the Joshua paradigm is given orders, he always has an active part to play in the battle, e.g., "you shall hamstring their horses, and burn their chariots with fire" (Josh 11:6). But Israel's role, like that of a king, has now been reduced to nothing. Israel is told concerning her foes in 41:12,

> You shall seek those who contend with you,
>> but you shall not find them;
> those who war against you
>> shall be as nothing at all.

In the coming battle Israel will not hamstring horses or burn chariots with fire because there will be no enemies to fight. The theme of the nullity of the enemies has already been introduced into the text in 40:17 and is matched by the related theme that the gods are nothing (see, e.g., 41:24). The orders given to the community here are like the community's orders in 2 Chr 20:17, "You will not need to fight in this battle."

Israel will not fight in the coming war of liberation because Yahweh will fight for the community. It has already been announced in 41:2 that Yahweh has "stirred up one from the east" (העיר ממזרח) to fight his battles. Yahweh is fighting through Cyrus to liberate his people. Israel is not to be actively engaged in war as was Joshua, but like a king the community is ordered to stay out of the battle.

What, then, is Israel's vocation, if Israel is not to be engaged in the battle that will result in her liberation? The answer to the question appears in the Orders given in the second pericope (41:14-16). The imagery in these verses, however, has often proved baffling to scholars. The problems are as follows: Why is Israel called a "worm" (תולעה)? How is its parallel word (מתי) to be translated? What does it mean that Israel is a "threshing sledge" (מורג חרוץ)? The task that Israel is to perform—"threshing" (דוש), "crushing" (דקק), "making like chaff" (כמץ שים) and "winnowing" (זרה)—fits into the notion of Israel as a "threshing sledge," but why is Israel to do these things to "mountains" (הרים) and "hills" (גבעות) rather than to grain? The imagery of the poetry in the opening of the book is an important consideration. That Israel's role is not that of a conventional warrior is evident from the preceding Orders (41:11-13) and also in Isa 40:9-11 where the phrase "fear not" occurs for the first time and in connection with a mention of Israel's task. Here Israel's role is to be a "herald of good tidings," i.e., to announce the victory of Yahweh.

> Get you up to a high mountain,
>> O Zion, herald of good tidings (מבשרת);
> lift up your voice with strength,
>> O Jerusalem, herald of good tidings (מבשרת),

lift it up, fear not (אל תיראי);
say to the cities of Judah,
   "Behold your God!"
Behold, the Lord GOD comes with might,
   and his arm rules for him;
behold his reward is with him,
   and his recompense before him,
He will feed his flock like a shepherd,
   he will gather the lambs in his arms,
he will carry them in his bosom,
   and gently lead those that are with young.

—Isa 40:9-11

Interestingly, this same theme follows shortly after the War Oracles in Isa 41 where Yahweh says "I will make[16] Jerusalem a herald of good tidings" (ולירושלם מבשר אהגו, 41:27). There the news to be heralded is Yahweh's victory through his warrior whom he describes in 41:25,

I stirred up from the north, and he has come,
   from the rising of the sun, and he shall call on my name;
he shall trample on rulers as on mortar,
   as the potter treads clay.

But why does he call Jacob/Israel a תולעת and מתי? These words emphasize the insignificance of Jacob/Israel.[17] Indeed, to be a "herald of good tidings" was a role customarily reserved for women[18] and was thus, given traditional attitudes toward women, unimportant for a would-be warrior. That Israel feels insignificant has already been noted earlier in the text in 40:27-31 where Israel is quoted as complaining, "My way is hid from the Lord, and my right is disregarded by my God" (Isa 40:27b). That Israel's role is not trivial, however, is suggested by the Basis of Assurance which says that Yahweh has made Israel a "threshing sledge" which will make mountains and hills into chaff. Again the meaning of this imagery is to be determined from the preceding poetry. In the Prologue we are told:

A voice cries:
"In the wilderness prepare the way of the LORD,
   make straight in the desert a highway for our God.
Every valley shall be lifted up,
   and every mountain and hill be made low;
the uneven ground shall become level,
   and the rough places a plain.

> And the glory of the LORD shall be revealed,
>
> and all flesh shall see it together,
>
> for the mouth of the LORD has spoken."

> —Isa 40:3-5

While it is uncertain in the Prologue who will "prepare the way of the LORD" and who will lift up every valley and make every mountain (הר) and hill (גבעה) low, the Orders in 41:15b-16 make it clear that Israel will do this. Yahweh now says to Jacob/Israel: "you shall thresh the mountains and crush them, and you shall make the hills like chaff." But how can we account for the odd language of "threshing," "crushing," "making into chaff" and "winnowing?" This language is used because it is characteristic war language to refer to destroying an enemy.[19] The only change is that Israel's participation is no longer directed against the enemy in the ensuing battle. Israel is to prepare and announce the victory of Yahweh in the triumphant march to Jerusalem. "Mountains" and "hills" should be understood to refer to the general obstacles standing in the way of Israel's return.[20] Israel as the "herald of good tidings" will overcome the hardships that she will meet when she returns on the glorious victory march with Yahweh. It is in the sense of Israel as the "herald of good tidings" that we should understand the last line of the orders (41:16b), "And you (ואתה) shall rejoice (הגיל) in the LORD; in the Holy One of Israel you shall glory (תתהלל)."[21]

The remaining part of the chapter (41:17-29) continues to develop the themes associated with Yahweh's address to the community as a warrior. Describing the fertility Yahweh will give to the desert, vss. 17-20 allude not only to the highway to be built for Yahweh's victory march (40:3ff.) but also to the orders given to the community to overcome the difficulties on the return home. Israel will be able to overcome the hardships because Yahweh will make the wilderness a fertile and inviting place. A trial scene in vss. 21-29 recalls the earlier trial scene in 41:1-4 and indicates that the gods are nothing and that the one who chooses the gods of the nations is an abomination. It testifies to the fact that Yahweh is the power behind the new conquerer and that the community will be the herald of good tidings announcing Yahweh's victory.

Links with Abraham in Isa 41:8-16

Earlier we noted that while the nations were busy "choosing" (בחר) good material to construct their gods, Israel/Jacob, Yahweh's servant, is addressed as one whom Yahweh has chosen (בחרתיך). The Address further identifies the community as "the offspring of Abraham my friend" (זרע אברהם אהבי), 41:8. The chosen regal community is, therefore, linked specifically with Abraham. Indeed, in 2 Chr 20:7 Jehoshaphat also identifies the community whom Yahweh addresses as a regal warrior as "the descendants of Abraham your friend" (לזרע אברהם אהבך). The association of the community with the patriarchs will become increasingly dominant in the remaining "fear not" texts to be examined. The community is not linked with the community of conquest at the time of Joshua but with the patriarchs. Other texts in Second Isaiah associate the election of the community with the patriarch Abraham (see 51:1-2)[22] and indeed 41:9 is probably to be associated with the call of Abraham.[23] The community is identified as

> you whom I took from the ends of the earth,
> and called from its farthest corners,
> saying to you, "You are my servant,
> I have chosen you and not cast you off."

An association with Abraham is likely because patriarchal traditions, as we will see in the next chapters, are closely linked with the language of address to a warrior used in connection with the exilic and post-exilic communities. We will also argue in Chapter VII that in Genesis the patriarchs are addressed as royal warriors of Yahweh.

According to the testimony that Yahweh gives in the trial scene Yahweh had declared his intentions from the beginning to Zion/Jerusalem. We will argue below that this declaration at the beginning is to be understood as the promise which Yahweh made to the patriarchs, and it is for that reason that Yahweh designates the community in 41:8-16 as the offspring of Abraham, i.e., as inheritors of the promise. It is also tempting to suggest that the "Servant Song" that follows in 42:1-4 with its royal connotations[24] continues the theme of 41:8-16 where Yahweh addresses the community as a king.

It will be helpful to summarize our discussion of the two units, 41:8-16. We have argued the following: (1) that the two units, 41:8-13 and 41:14-16, follow the stereotypical language of address to a warrior; (2) that the use of the genre parallels the conventions associated with the address to the king as warrior; (3) that as a king the community will not have a battle to fight but will be a herald of good tidings announcing the victory of Yahweh; and (4) that the regal community is specifically identified as the offspring of Abraham. If this is the case, the patriarchal and royal traditions are linked poetically, and theories associating the patriarchs and kings are reinforced.

War Oracles Addressed to a King: the Structure of Isa 43:1-7 and 44:1-5

These two units also follow the conventions of the War Oracle when it is used to address a king.[25] Those who understand these texts as Oracles of Salvation usually break Isa 43:1-7 into two units: 43:1-4 and 43:5-7. For our discussion we will follow this procedure although the War Oracle when it is used to address a king is sometimes extended by the recurrence of structural elements so that it would be equally possible to take 43:1-7 as one unit. The structure of the texts can be outlined as follows:

Isa 43:1-4

(a)   PROPHETIC MESSENGER FORMULA

> But now thus says the LORD,
>   he who created you, O Jacob,
>   he who formed you, O Israel:
> ועתה כה אמר יהוה בראך יעקב
>   ויצרך ישראל

(b)   ASSURANCE

> "Fear not,
> אל תירא

(c)   BASIS OF ASSURANCE

> for I have redeemed you;
>   I have called you by name, you are mine.
> When you pass through the waters I will be with you;
>   and through the rivers, they shall not overwhelm you;
> when you walk through fire you shall not be burned,
>   and the flame shall not consume you.
> For I am the LORD your God,
>   the Holy One of Israel, your Savior.
> כי גאלתיך קראתי בשמך לי אתה
> כי תעבר במים אתך אני ובנהרות לא ישטפוך
> כי תלך במו אש לא תכוה ולהבה לא תבער בך
> כי אני יהוה אלהיך קדוש ישראל מושיעך

(d)   PROMISE

> I give Egypt as your ransom,
>   Ethiopia and Seba in exchange for you.
> Because you are precious in my eyes,
>   and honored, and I love you.
> I give men in return for you,

peoples in exchange for your life.

נתתי כפרך מצרים כוש וסבא תחתיך
מאשר יקרת בעיני נכבדת ואני אהבתיך
ואתן אדם תחתיך ולאמים תחת נפשך

Isa 43:5-7

(a)   ASSURANCE

Fear not,
אל תירא

(b)   BASIS OF ASSURANCE

for I am with you;
כי אתך אני

(c)   PROMISE

I will bring your offspring from the east,
   and from the west I will gather you;
I will say to the north, Give up,
   and to the south, Do not withhold;
bring my sons from afar
   and my daughters from the end of the earth,
every one who is called by my name,
   whom I created for my glory,
   whom I formed and made."

ממזרח אביא זרעך וממערב אקבצך
אמר לצפון תני ולתימן אל תכלאי
הביאי בני מרחוק ובנותי מקצה הארץ
כל הנקרא בשמי ולכבודי בראתיו יצרתיו
אף עשיתיו

Isa 44:1-5

(a)   ADDRESS

But how hear, O Jacob my servant,
   Israel whom I have chosen!
ועתה שמע יעקב עבדי וישראל בחרהי בו

(b)   PROPHETIC MESSENGER FORMULA

Thus says the LORD who made you,
   who formed you from the womb
   and will help you:
כה אמר יהוה עשך ויצרך מבטן יעזרך

(c)   ASSURANCE

"Fear not,
אל תירא

(d)   ADDRESS

O Jacob my servant,
   Jeshurun whom I have chosen.
עבדי יעקב וישרון בחרתי בו

(e)   PROMISE
For I will pour water on the thirsty land,
   and streams on the dry ground;

I will pour my Spirit upon your descendants,
   and my blessing on your offspring.
They shall spring up like grass amid waters,
   like willows by flowing streams.
This one will say, 'I am the LORD's,'
   another will call himself by the name of Jacob,
and another will write on his hand, 'The LORD's,'
   and surname himself by the name of Israel."

כי אצק מים על צמא ונזלים על יבשה
אצק רוחי על זרעך וברכתי על צאצאיך
וצמחו בבין חציר כערבים על יבלי מים
זה יאמר ליהוה אני וזה יקרא בשם יעקב
וזה יכהב ידו ליהוה ובשם ישראל יכנה

These texts also conform to the conventions of the War Oracle when it is used to address a king. The Assurance is אל תירא. As is typical of Second Isaiah's use of the genre, there is no Object of Fear. The Basis of Assurance in 43:1-4 and 43:5-7 is introduced by כי and in both places the theme of Yahweh's presence "with" (את) the recipient of the oracle occurs. In 43:1-4, however, the Basis of Assurance is longer than is normally the case; there are four lines all introduced by the particle כי. (In 41:8-13 we noted that the Basis of Assurance was also longer than usual and was repeated at the end of the unit.) There is no Basis of Assurance in 44:1-5 although the second Address supports the phrase "fear not," and the Promise, uncharacteristically introduced by כי, acts as a kind of Basis of Assurance. Unlike the two oracles in 41:8-16, each of these three units has a Promise rather than Orders. When a War Oracle is spoken to a king, the deity will sometimes announce in the first person a Promise concerning the coming battle rather than give the king Orders (compare, e.g., Isa 37:6//2 Kgs 19:6 and our analysis of the extra-biblical oracles in Chapter III). The prophetic messenger formula in 43:1 and 44:2 occurred in conjunction with the War Oracle in other uses of the genre associated with kingship (compare Isa 7:7 and 2 Chr 20:15). The use of the Address which occurs twice in 44:1-5 is characteristic of the War Oracle spoken to a king, and the Address in 44:1 containing a summons to hear (שמע) has also occurred before (see Deut 20:3 and 2 Chr 20:15). Structurally, then, these texts fit the conventions of the War Oracle addressed to a king.

The Literary Contexts of the Royal War Oracles in Isa 43:1-7 and 44:1-5

Why would Second Isaiah use the War Oracle addressed to a king in 43:1-7 and 44:1-5, and what is the *Sitz im Text*? The point of departure for answering this question is found in the phrase which opens each of the units, "but now" (ועתה).[26] This phrase is a clue not only to the *Sitz im Text* but to the structure of the genre, which uses a Promise rather than Orders. We noted that in 41:8-16 the phrase, "but you" (ואתה), introduced War Oracles that contained Orders given to "you" Israel and set up a contrast between the activity of Israel in the coming war and the activities of the nations described in 41:5-7. In 43:1-7 and 44:1-5 the "but now" introduces the activity of Yahweh announced in the Promise and contrasts the new activity of Yahwah with his former activity described in 42:18-25 and 43:22-28.

The *Sitz im Text* of the War Oracles in 43:1-7 and 44:1-5 are similar. (1) Immediately before the War Oracles Yahweh defends himself in polemics against his people by arguing that they have failed and for that reason he has judged them and delivered them to the enemy. Form critics have identified the two units (42:18-25 and 43:22-28), which precede the two War Oracles, as trial speeches of Yahweh against Israel.[27] The trial speeches, we will argue, function in a way similar to that of the disputation in 40:27-31 which preceded the War Oracles in 41:8-16, i.e., Yahweh seeks to persuade the community by defending himself against the claims that he had deserted them.[28] (2) In both 43:1-7 and 44:1-5 the War Oracles are introduced by the phrase, "but now" (ועתה), signaling a change in Yahweh's actions concerning his people. Whereas Yahweh had militarily defeated his people for their own failures, the War Oracles indicate that Yahweh will *now* fight for his people to deliver them. The point has already been made in chapter 41 that Yahweh is the power behind the conqueror Cyrus. (3) Following the War Oracles are trial speeches against the nations (43:8-13 and 44:6-8) in which three points are made: (a) that there is no god but Yahweh, who is in control of things, and that therefore the nations have no defense, (b) that Yahweh has declared formerly or long ago the things to come, and (c) that the people (Jacob/Israel) are Yahweh's witnesses.

The War Oracles in 43:1-7 and in 44:1-5, then, have a similar *Sitz im Text*; in both places Jacob/Israel is comforted and assured that Yahweh will *now* fight on his behalf. Having spoken generally about the *Sitz im Text*, it will now be helpful to look more specifically at the War Oracles and their setting.

First, let us consider the two War Oracles in 43:1-7 which are preceded by a trial speech against Israel (42:18-25). The trial scene opens with Yahweh summoning the deaf to hear and the blind to look and see (42:18), and proceeds to disputation questions:

> Who is blind but my servant,
>> or deaf as my messenger whom I send?
> Who is blind as my dedicated one,
>> or blind as the servant of the LORD?[29]

—Isa 42:19

According to C. Westermann this trial speech, which has baffled commentators, needs to be read in conjunction with the disputation in 40:27-31.[30] Those verses indicate clearly that Jacob/Israel has challenged Yahweh with the following questions:

> Why do you say, O Jacob,
>> and speak, O Israel,
> "My way is hid from the LORD,
>> and my right is disregarded by my God?"

—Isa 40:27

Westermann argues that these questions amount to Jacob/Israel charging that Yahweh is blind and deaf to the community's present plight. He further contends that in the trial speech in 42:18-25 Yahweh is arguing that it is not he but Jacob/Israel who is deaf and blind. Our interpretation of the War Oracles in 41:8-16 adds another dimension to Westermann's argument. We argued that in the War Oracles in 41:8-16 Jacob/Israel was given orders to be a "herald of good tidings" announcing the victory of Yahweh. This disputation (42:18-25) also picks up the motif of Jacob/Israel's task by alluding to the fact that the servant is a messenger (מלאך 42:19). In this disputation Yahweh seeks to set the situation straight so that his messenger can understand.

In the trial speech it is acknowledged that Jacob/Israel is a defeated people,

> But this is a people robbed and plundered,
>> they are all of them trapped in holes
>> and hidden in prisons;
> they have become a prey with none to rescue,
>> a spoil with none to say, "restore!"

—Isa 42:22

Indeed, it might appear that Yahweh is deaf and blind, but according to vs. 23 the situation is quite different for any one who will only listen to the facts. Although Yahweh was responsible for handing the people over to the spoiler and to robbers, it was because the people had sinned and had not been obedient to the law. This confession is made by the prophet himself in vs. 24 when he identifies with the community and says,

> Was it not the LORD against whom we have sinned,
>   in whose ways they would not walk,
>   and whose law they would not obey?

—Isa 42:24

It is important to observe that Yahweh's judgment of the people is described as a military defeat for which Yahweh was solely responsible.

> So he (Yahweh) poured upon him (Jacob) the heat of his anger
>   and the might of battle (ועזוז מלחמה);
> it set him on fire round about, but he did not understand;
>   it burned him, but he did not take it to heart.

—Isa 42:25

It is precisely at this point that the War Oracles in 43:1-7 are introduced into the text with the important linking phrase, "but now" (ועתה). This phrase suggests the contrast between Yahweh's former judgment of the people through military defeat and the new promise of victory to the community in the War Oracles in 43:1-7. The Basis of Assurance in 43:1b-3 is the antithesis of Yahweh's former battle against his people, described in 42:25. Jacob/Israel is to "fear not"

> for I (Yahweh) have redeemed you;
>   I have called you by name, you are mine.
> When you pass through the waters I will be with you;
>   and through the rivers, they shall not overwhelm you;
> when you walk through fire you shall not be burned,
>   and the flame shall not consume you.
> For I am the LORD your God,
>   the Holy One of Israel, your savior.

In the former war (42:25) Yahweh had turned against Jacob/Israel so that the battle set him on fire (ותלהטהו) and burned him (ותבער בו). In this War Oracle, however, Yahweh assures Jacob/Israel that he is now with (את) him so that he shall walk through fire (אש) and not be burned (לא תכוה), so that he will not be consumed (לא תבער) by the flame (להבה). In our discussion of the structure of this unit we noted that the Basis of Assurance was longer than is generally the case. It is the sharp polarity between the former situation of defeat and the new situation of victory that helps explain the extended length of this Basis of Assurance.

The function of the two War Oracles in 43:1-7, then, is to assure Jacob/Israel that Yahweh, who in the past had poured out "the heat of his anger" and "the might of battle"

against him, will now fight for him in battle. Two other observations need to be made
about the content of the War Oracles in 43:1-7: (1) The War Oracles emphasize the fact
that it was Yahweh who created Jacob/Israel,

> But now thus says the LORD,
>> he who created (בראך) you, O Jacob
>> he who formed (יצרך) you, O Israel.

—Isa 43:1a

and

>> every one who is called by my name,
>> whom I created (בראתיו) for my glory
>> whom I formed (יצרתיו) and made (עשיתיו).

—Isa 43:7

How are we to understand this language concerning the forming, creating and making of
Jacob/Israel? Is it referring to any particular period in the Israelite tradition concerning
the creation of the community, Jacob/Israel? (2) In the War Oracles, Yahweh promises
his people that he will rescue them. In the second oracle, the promise is that those to be
rescued are the "offspring" (זרע) of Jacob/Israel. Why is there this emphasis on
offspring? These questions concerning the creation of Jacob/Israel and the rescue of the
offspring are also prominent in the oracle in 44:1-5, and they will be answered in
conjunction with that discussion.

The trial speech against the nations in 43:8-13, which follows the War Oracles in
43:1-7, functions to prove the power of Yahweh to deliver his people; in comparison with
Yahweh the gods of the nations are nothing. In this way the trial speech is like the trial
speech in 41:1-4 associated with the War Oracles in 41:8-16; only Yahweh is god, and it is
Yahweh who controls the rise to power of the conqueror Cyrus. There are two major
motifs in the trial speech in 43:8-13. The significance of these motifs will also be
discussed later, in conjunction with the trial speech against the nations in 44:22-28 where
similar motifs occur. The motifs are: (1) The nations are challenged by Yahweh to
declare (נגד) what Yahweh is declaring, i.e., to make known the former things (ראשנות),
43:9. Whereas the nations cannot declare, Yahweh says, "I declared (הגדתי) and saved
(והושעתי) and proclaimed (והשמעתי)," 43:12. When did Yahweh declare and proclaim what
the nations cannot, and what are the former things? (2) While the gods cannot bring
forth "their witnesses" (עדיהם), 43:9, Yahweh twice says to the community "you are my

witnesses" (אתם עדי), 43:10,12. How are we to understand the community as witnesses of Yahweh? On what basis is the community to be Yahweh's witnesses?

Before answering the questions we raised concerning motifs associated with the War Oracles in 43:1-7 and the following trial speech against the nations in 43:8-13, it will be necessary to examine the content of the Oracle in 44:1-5 and its context. We noted above that the War Oracle in 44:1-5 is preceded by a trial speech against Israel (43:22-28). In the trial speech Yahweh accuses the people of not calling upon him in worship but of wearying him with their sins. It is important to note here the seriousness of Israel's sin. The failure of Jacob/Israel is traced to the beginning.

> Your first father sinned,
> and your mediators transgressed against me.

>   —Isa 43:27

Here the first father refers to the patriarch Jacob in a tradition similar to the Jacob tradition in Hos 12:3-5. Second Isaiah, like Ezekiel (cf. Ezek 20), is saying that from the very beginning the community transgressed against Yahweh. This trial speech deepens the charge Yahweh made against Jacob/Israel in the trial speech in 42:18-25 which had resulted in the defeat of the people in battle. The last verse in the trial speech, vs. 28, picks up language associated with war.

> Therefore I profaned (ואחלל) the princes of the
> sanctuary,
> I delivered Jacob to utter destruction (לחרם)
> and Israel to reviling (לגדופים).

When Yahweh says he profaned (חלל) the princes of the sanctuary, he is using the word, חלל, as he used it in Isa 47:6 to speak about profaning his people by giving them over to Babylon. The word חרם, as is well known, is used in contexts of war where the spoils of the enemy are devoted to the deity. The word, גדף, is also sometimes used in military contexts. This word is used in the War Oracle in Isa 37:6 (//2 Kgs 19:6) in the Object of Fear. Hezekiah is not to be afraid,

> because of the words that you have heard, with which the servants of
> the king of Assyria have reviled me (גדפו . . . אותי).

In this trial speech, then, Yahweh is defending himself by giving the reasons for delivering his people to military defeat. They were handed over to the enemy because even their first father had sinned.

Following this trial speech, the War Oracle (44:1-5), introduced by the phrase, ועתה,
signals a change in the situation. Yahweh is now comforting the community by
announcing that he will rescue his people and fight for them. This War Oracle contains
the two motifs found in the War Oracles in 43:1-7: (1) The community whom Yahweh has
chosen is described as being formed and made by Yahweh. The imagery of forming and
making Israel is here related to forming the community in the womb.

> Thus says the LORD who made you (עשך),
> who formed you (יצרך) from the womb
> and will help you.

—Isa 44:2

Again the question arises: How are we to understand this imagery of Yahweh forming
Jacob/Israel in the womb? (2) In this oracle, as in 43:1-7, Yahweh promises that it is the
"offspring" (זרע in parallel with צאצא) of Jacob/Israel who will be blessed and delivered
by Yahweh's victory, vs. 3. How are we to understand this emphasis on the restoration of
the offspring?

Following the War Oracle in 44:1-5 is a trial scene against the nations (44:6-8) which
contains the same two motifs found in the trial speech against the nations in 43:8-13.
Yahweh is defending himself against the gods of the nations by maintaining that only he
is god. His defense consists of two arguments: (1) He challenges the nations and their
gods to proclaim (קרא) and declare (נגד) and set forth (ערך) what is happening, to
announce from of old the things to come (מי השמיע מעולם אותיות) and to tell what is
to be (ואשר תבאנה יגידו למו). This is comparable to the challenge in the trial speech in
43:8-13 in which the gods are to declare the former things (ראשנות). Again the question
is raised: What are these former things that Yahweh can declare and the gods of the
nations cannot? (2) In this trial speech, as in 43:8-13, Yahweh says that, unlike the gods
of the nations, he has witnesses who can affirm what he declared long ago and witness to
what is yet to be.

> Fear not, nor be afraid;
>> have I not told you (השמעתיך) from of old (מאז)
>> and declared it (והגדתי)?
>> And you are my witnesses (עדי)!
> Is there a God besides me?
>> There is no Rock; I know not any."

—Isa 44:8

Here again the question arises: What does it mean that Israel is Yahweh's witnesses?

The two War Oracles in 43:1-7 and the War Oracle in 44:1-5 function similarly in their *Sitze im Text*. They comfort Jacob/Israel by assuring him that Yahweh will now fight for the community, reversing his past action of handing over his people to the enemy's destruction. We have still to answer questions concerning the two themes that are commonly raised in the two War Oracles and the two themes that are raised in the trial speeches against the nations that follow the War Oracles: (1) How are we to understand the emphasis on Yahweh creating Jacob/Israel in the womb? (2) Why is there an emphasis on the rescue of the "offspring?" (3) What does it mean that Jacob/Israel is Yahweh's witness? (4) How are we to understand the argument that Yahweh announced formerly (declared long ago) what is now about to take place? It is our argument that all but the last of these four questions can be partially answered by recognizing the conventions associated with the War Oracle when it is used to address a king. We further argue that these partial answers can be expanded and the final question answered by considering the way Second Isaiah is employing the genre to express his understanding of Israelite tradition.

Before dealing at length with the motifs of creation/formation in the womb and the rescue of offspring, let us briefly discuss the motif of the community as witnesses for Yahweh. We would argue that a link exists between the witnesses motif and the conventions associated with the War Oracle addressed to a king. The vocation of the community as witnesses for Yahweh, a theme found in the trial speeches against the nations, can clearly be associated with a royal office, at least in Second Isaiah's thought. Isa 55:3-5 has often been understood as a pericope in which the everlasting covenant promises to David have been transferred to the people. The people have become the king or have inherited the promises originally given to the king.[31] However, the community has not only received the promises but has also inherited the vocation of David, i.e., to be a witness to the nations,

> Incline your ear, and come to me;
>   hear, that your soul may live;
> and I will make with you an everlasting covenant,
>   my steadfast sure love for David.
> Behold, I made him a witness (עד) to the peoples,
>   a leader (נגיד) and commander (מצוה) of the peoples.

—Isa 55:3-4

Just as David was to be a witness for Yahweh to the nations, now the community is to assume that role. That is the task assigned Jacob/Israel in the trial speeches accompanying the War Oracles; the community is to be a witness for Yahweh. With such an understanding of the role of witness, it is appropriate for Second Isaiah to use the War Oracle as it is used to address a king.

What can be said about the motif of Yahweh creating Jacob/Israel and the emphasis on the offspring of the community--the two themes that occur in the War Oracles? We have noted that the theme of creating, forming, and making of Jacob/Israel in 43:1-7 is more fully described as making, forming, and creating Jacob/Israel from the womb (מבטן) in 44:1-5. We noted in our discussion of Jer 1,[32] where Yahweh addressed Jeremiah as a warrior, that Yahweh had appointed Jeremiah to his warrior vocation before the prophet was formed in the womb.

> Before I formed (אצורך) you in the womb (בבטן) I knew you,
>   and before you were born I consecrated you;
>   I appointed you a prophet to the nations.
>
> —Jer 1:5

There is precedent, then, for associating the language of war with the appointment of the warrior to his vocation before he was born. (In the case of Jeremiah, however, the genre is not used to address a non-combatant king but a warrior who is to be actively engaged in battle.) The motif of the deity's protection of the king from birth is particularly clear in Mesopotamian texts where the War Oracle is used to address a king.[33] Consider, for example, the following phrases which occur in the War Oracles addressed to Esarhaddon: Ishtar says to Esarhaddon in Oracle #3, "I watch over your inner heart as would your mother who brought you forth." In the same oracle she says, "When you were small I chose you."[34] The association of the deity's concern for the king from birth is stressed even more clearly in Oracle #4 where Ishtar says to Esarhaddon, "I am the great midwife (who helped at your birth), the one who gave you suck." In the same oracle she identifies Esarhaddon as "the son of the goddess Ninlil."[35] A similar theme is found in "An Oracular Dream concerning Ashurbanipal," where Ishtar is described as follows: "she spoke to you like the mother who bore you."[36] These Mesopotamian texts do not speak of forming the "warrior" in the womb as do Jer 1:5 and Isa 44:2, but they do emphasize the motif of the protection of the king from birth.

It is possible to understand the theme of the rescue of the "offspring" as being associated with the War Oracle when it is used to address a king. In Oracle #5 associated with Esarhaddon, the Queen mother is concerned about her offspring and complains to the deity.

> He who is at the right and he who is at the left you hold on your lap,
> but where is my offspring? You make him run about (unprotected) in
> the open country![37]

It is tempting to associate the birth of Immanuel in Isa. 7, which follows the War Oracle addressed to Ahaz, with concern for the offspring. Perhaps the War Oracle's expression of concern for the rescue of the offspring of the king is related to the promise of posterity for the king, i.e., the continuance of the dynasty. One way of understanding the two themes of the creation from the womb and the rescue of the offspring, then, is to interpret them in light of conventions associated with the War Oracle used to address a king. It is important to explore further these two themes, this time not from the perspective of the conventions associated with the royal War Oracle, but in the larger context of Second Isaiah's use of tradition. Let us look again in Isa 44:2 at the motif of Yahweh forming Jacob/Israel in the womb; this theme contraposes Yahweh's accusation in the previous trial speech against Israel that the community's first father Jacob had sinned. It has often been noted that the Jacob tradition in Second Isaiah (Isa 43:27) is closely associated with the Jacob tradition in Hos 12:2-6.[38] In both places the Jacob tradition is understood negatively and the actions of Jacob are the basis of a trial or legal dispute Yahweh has with the community, the descendants of Jacob. We have already looked at the trial scene in Second Isaiah. The trial scene in Hosea, which follows, helps illuminate the motif in Isaiah of Jacob/Israel being formed from the womb.

> The LORD has an indictment against Judah,
>   and will punish Jacob according to his ways,
>   and requite him according to his deeds.
> In the womb (בבטן) he took his brother by the heel,
>   and in his manhood he strove with God.
> He strove with the angel and prevailed,
>   he wept and sought his favor.
> He met God at Bethel,
>   and there God spoke with him —
> the LORD the God of hosts,
>   the LORD is his name.

—Hos 12:3-5

The important thing to note here is not only that Hosea, like Second Isaiah, uses the actions of the man Jacob as an indictment against the community descended from Jacob, but that in Hosea there is the tradition of the sin having originated in the womb, when Jacob "took his brother by the heel." We would argue that the tradition concerning the struggle of Jacob in the womb (cf. Gen 25:23) helps explain the allusion to Yahweh's forming Jacob/Israel in the womb in Isa 44:2. It was in the womb that Yahweh formed the community that now bears that ancestor's name, and it is in the womb that Jacob first sinned. In 44:1-5 Yahweh is addressing the community formed in the womb concerning his new resolve to deliver Jacob; the allusion to the original formation in the womb refers to a time before the first father sinned and thus suggests an obliteration of that past sin and Yahweh's past judgment.

The use of patriarchal traditions in Second Isaiah's thought, however, extends beyond this one tradition associated with Jacob who sinned against Yahweh. It will be recalled in the War Oracle in Isa 41:8-16 that Jacob/Israel was identified as "the offspring of Abraham, my friend" (זרע אברהם אהבי). It is our contention that Jacob/Israel as the offspring of Abraham is the inheritor of the promises first given to Abraham that he would be the father of a great posterity (cf. Gen 15:1-6).[39] Such a patriarchal tradition helps explain the motif in the War Oracles concerning the rescue of the offspring. One pericope in Second Isaiah, 48:18-19, alludes to the unfulfilled promise of abundant offspring. Yahweh says to the community,

> O that you had hearkened to my commandments!
>   Then your peace would have been like a river,
>   and your righteousness like the waves of the sea;
> your offspring (זרעך) would have been like the sand,
>   and your descendants (צאצאי מעיך) like its grains;[40]
> their name (שמו) would never be cut off
>   or destroyed from before me.

The reference to the offspring "like the sand" is an allusion to the promise to the patriarchs that guaranteed them a great posterity, an offspring as numerous as the sand on the seashore,

> And the angel of the LORD called to Abraham a second time from heaven, and said, "By myself I have sworn, says the LORD, because you have done this, and have not withheld your son, your only son, I will indeed bless you, and I will multiply your descendants (זרעך) as

the stars of the heaven and as the sand which is on the seashore. And
your descendants shall possess the gate of their enemies, and by your
descendants shall all the nations of the earth bless themselves,
because you have obeyed my voice.

—Gen 22:15-18

The promise of offspring in this passage entails possession of the gate of their enemies by
the descendants and the blessing of the nations through the descendants. According to
Isa 48:19, if Jacob/Israel had hearkened to Yahweh's commandments, Jacob/Israel's name
would not have been cut off or destroyed. This also picks up a theme from the
patriarchal promises. For example in Gen 12:2 Yahweh promises that he will make
Abraham's name great (ואגדלה שמך). Isa 48:18-19, then, suggests that, if Jacob/Israel
had been obedient, the promises to the patriarchs would have been fulfilled.

The War Oracles suggest that there will be a new beginning and that the patriarchal
promises will be fulfilled. Yahweh had delivered his people to destruction in battle, but
now he will fight for his people and deliver their offspring. In the War Oracles in Isa
43:1-7, Yahweh, promising that he will give peoples in exchange for Jacob/Israel (vss. 3-
4), says that he will gather the offspring from the four corners of the earth (vss. 5-6).
The offspring are those who are called by Yahweh's name (vs. 7). Likewise in the War
Oracle in Isa 44:1-5, Yahweh promises that he will pour his spirit on the descendants
(זרע) of Jacob/Israel and bless their offspring (צאצאיך) and that they will be so numerous
that they will spring up like grass amid waters and like willows by flowing streams (vss.3-
4). Furthermore, this people will now have a name,

> This one will say, "I am the LORD's"
> another will call himself by the name (בשם) of Jacob,
> and another will write on his hand, "The LORD's"
> and surname himself by the name of Israel.

—Isa 44:5

The War Oracles in 43:1-7 and in 44:1-5, then, not only draw on conventions
associated with the oracle when it is used to address a king; they also emphasize the
importance of patriarchal traditions in Second Isaiah's understanding of Israelite
history. It is as the offspring of Abraham, Yahweh's friend, that Yahweh addresses the
community as king. Although even Israel's first father, Jacob, sinned, and although
Yahweh had delivered his people to destruction at the hands of their enemies, Yahweh
now announces that he will restore the community and assure the people of abundant

offspring.

Having dealt with three motifs in the War Oracles (Jacob/Israel as witness, creation of Jacob/Israel in the womb, and rescue of offspring) how can we understand the fourth motif? Second Isaiah's understanding of history helps us answer the fourth question that we raised concerning the "former things" and the things announced by Yahweh long ago which are a clue to what is yet to come. Earlier in the chapter we argued that the War Oracles in 43:1-7 and the War Oracle in 44:1-5 have a similar textual setting. They are preceded by an argument of Yahweh stating why it is that Jacob/Israel has been delivered into the hand of the enemy, and they are followed by trial speeches in which Yahweh argues that the nations do not know the former things and cannot declare what he had announced long ago. Isa 43:14-21 is a significant unit linking the two War Oracles (43:1-7 and 44:1-5) with their surrounding contexts, and must be examined in order to further unravel Second Isaiah's understanding of tradition. The unit opens with the prophetic messenger formula, "Thus says the LORD" (vs. 14). The message is one of salvation and describes the present, the now, which is the subject of each of the War Oracles. Yahweh will defeat Babylon and effect the liberation of his people.

> For your sake I will send to Babylon
> and break down all the bars
> and the shouting of the Chaldeans will be turned to
> lamentation.[41]

—Isa 43:14

The Lord who delivers them now is described using the imagery of Yahweh's military defeat of the Egyptians, when he delivered his people at the sea,

> Thus says the LORD,
> who makes a way in the sea
> a path in the mighty waters,
> who brings forth chariot and horse,
> army and warrior;
> they lie down, they cannot rise,
> they are extinguished, quenched like a wick.

—Isa 43:16-17

The imagery used to describe Yahweh who is promising a new Exodus of the community from Babylon echoes Yahweh's promise when he called Moses to lead his people out of the land of Egypt.

Say therefore to the people of Israel, "I am the LORD, and I will
bring you out from under the burdens of the Egyptians, and I will
redeem you with an outstretched arm and with great acts of
judgment, and I will take you for my people, and I will be your God;
and you shall know that I am the LORD your God, who has brought
you out from under the burdens of the Egyptians. And I will bring
you into the land which I swore to give to Abraham, to Isaac, and to
Jacob; I will give it to you for a possession. I am the LORD.

--Exod 6:6-8

In the message of salvation, however, Jacob/Israel is exhorted by Yahweh not to
remember this past act of deliverance, for Yahweh is doing a new thing,

Remember not the former things (ראשנות),
    nor consider the things of old (קדמניות).
Behold I am doing a new thing:
    Now it springs forth, do you not perceive it?
I will make a way in the wilderness
    and rivers in the desert.
The wild beasts will honor me,
    the jackals and the ostriches;
for I give water in the wilderness,

    rivers in the desert,
to give drink to my chosen people,
    the people whom I formed for myself
that they might declare my praise.

—Isa 43:18-21

Yahweh's deliverance was followed ultimately by Israel's defeat at the hand of the
enemy. This defeat, however, did not mean that Israel's way was hid from Yahweh (Isa
40:27) or that Yahweh was impotent for, as the arguments preceding the War Oracles
show, it was Israel's disobedience that led to defeat. Even Israel's first father had
sinned. Yahweh is now doing a new thing to deliver his people. The deliverance
described here (43:19-21) alludes to Israel's Orders given in the former War Oracles in
41:8-16. Yahweh will help Israel overcome the hardships of the desert so that
Jacob/Israel as the herald of good tidings can proclaim Yahweh's praise in the victory
march to the homeland.

Second Isaiah's assessment of Israel's history (like that of Ezekiel in Ezek 20) as a
failure helps explain the importance of patriarchal traditions in his thought. Although
Second Isaiah draws on Exodus imagery in his vision of Yahweh's deliverance of the exiles

from Babylon,[42] it is the promise to Abraham and not a past deliverance of Israel that assures him of the imminent Exodus of the exiles from Babylon. Yahweh's promise declared long ago is still in force for the exilic community. Although Israel's offspring is threatened by exile, Yahweh is now acting to fulfill his promise. Israel as the inheritor of that promise—having experienced the former acts of deliverance which had ended in failure because of Israel's sin—can be Yahweh's witnesses. From the perspective of the tradition that Israel had been formed in the patriarchal days of Abraham and Sarah (cf. Isa 51:1-2), to whom a numerous offspring was promised, the rise of Cyrus to power makes sense because Yahweh is acting through Cyrus to gather his people and increase their offspring.

Summary

Our analysis of the "fear not" texts in Second Isaiah has indicated that he uses royal War Oracles. Second Isaiah uses two basic forms of the War Oracle addressed to a king. In 41:8-16 the War Oracles contain Orders. As is typical of the Orders in a royal War Oracle, the orders do not instruct Jacob/Israel to become actively engaged in the fighting. Kings do not fight; the deity fights for them. Jacob/Israel's orders are to be a herald of good tidings announcing the victory of Yahweh on the victory march to Jerusalem. The oracles in 43:1-7 and in 44:1-5 contain a Promise rather than Orders. Here Yahweh in the first person promises that he will achieve the victory for the regal community.

In Second Isaiah, then, the community has become the king for whom Yahweh fights. The War Oracles and their textual setting give insight into Second Isaiah's understanding of the exilic community in light of Israel's past history. The patriarch Abraham is the paradigm for understanding the regal community in relation to the rise of the conqueror Cyrus. The trial speeches are intended to show that it is Yahweh alone, not the gods of the nations, who is behind the imminent victory of this new warrior on the world scene. Israel should know this because Israel is the offspring of Abraham, Yahweh's friend. Israel's history had ended in failure and the roots of that failure extend to Jacob who had sinned against Yahweh. Still Yahweh had chosen Jacob/Israel and formed him in the womb to be his servant. While Israel's history had been a failure, Yahweh's promise to Abraham is still valid. Yahweh had promised Abraham that he would make his offspring as numerous as the grains of sand by the sea. When Yahweh gathers the offspring of Jacob/Israel and increases them abundantly, they can witness to the fulfillment of Yahweh's promise which he had first made to Abraham long ago. While there is no longer a Davidic king (Isa 53:3-5) to be Yahweh's witness, the restored community which Yahweh will redeem through the victory of Cyrus will be a royal community in the world of nations.

CHAPTER VI

PROTO-APOCALYPTIC ESCHATOLOGY AND THE ANCESTRAL PROMISE

Introduction

In this chapter we will discuss three passages (1) Jer 30:10-11 closely paralleled by Jer 46:27-28, (2) Zeph 3:16-18a, and (3) Isa 10:24-27. The structure of these texts suggest that they are War Oracles which are used, as in Second Isaiah, to address the community as king. Furthermore, the *Sitze im Text* of these oracles have parallels with the way the "fear not" oracles function in their textual setting in Second Isaiah.

Jer 30:10-11 and 46:27-28

These two texts are very nearly a word-for-word parallel of one another. Although there are minor variations, the texts are so closely related to one another that it is impossible to conceive that they were written independently. Either one of the texts is a variation of the other, which was original, or they are both variations of an oracle that no longer exists. Structurally, one might argue for Jer 46:27-28 to contain the more original or authentic form.[1] The extra "fear not" in 46:27-28 makes it possible to divide the unit into two distinct War Oracles attached to one another as in Isa 41:8-16 and 43:1-7. Jer 30:10-11 with only one "fear not" is more like a single War Oracle with recurring elements. Whatever the case may be, these two texts provide an interesting opportunity to test a methodological point that we have been making throughout the study, i.e., that the identification of a genre is often a clue to the meaning of its textual setting. The textual settings are different but both *Sitze im Text* are appropriate settings for War Oracles.

The two texts can be outlined as follows:

Jer 30:10-11

(a) ADDRESS

    But you,
    ואתה

(b) ASSURANCE

    fear not,
    אל תירא

(c) ADDRESS

> O Jacob my servant,
> עבדי יעקב

(d) ORACULAR FORMULA

> says the LORD,
> נאם יהוה

(e) ASSURANCE

> nor be dismayed,
> ואל תחת

(f) ADDRESS

> O Israel;
> ישראל

(g) PROMISE

> for lo, I will save you from afar,
>   and your offspring from the land of their
>   captivity.
> Jacob will return and have quiet and ease,
>   and none shall make him afraid.
> כי הנני מושיעך מרחוק ואת זרעך מארץ שבים
> ושב יעקב ושקט ושאנן ואין מחריד

(h) BASIS OF ASSURANCE

> For I am with you,
> כי אתך אני

(i) ORACULAR FORMULA

> says the Lord,
> נאם יהוה

(j) PROMISE

> to save you.
> I will make a full end of all nations
>   among whom I scattered you,
>   but of you I will not make a full end.
> I will chasten you in just measure,
>   and I will by no means leave you unpunished.
> להושיעך
> כי אעשה כלה בכל הגוים אשר הפצותיך שם
> אך אתך לא אעשה כלה ויסרתיך למשפט ונקה לא אנקך

Jer 46:27

(a) ADDRESS

> But you,
> ואתה

(b)   ASSURANCE

      fear not,
      אל תירא

(c)   ADDRESS

      O Jacob my servant,
      עבדי יעקב

(d)   ASSURANCE

      nor be dismayed,
      ואל תחת

(e)   ADDRESS

      O Israel;
      ישראל

(f)   PROMISE

      for lo, I will save you from afar,
        and your offspring from the land
          of their captivity.
      Jacob shall return and have quiet and ease,
      and none shall make him afraid.
      כי הנני מושעך מרחוק ואת זרעך מארץ שבים
        ושב יעקב ושקט ושאנן ואין מחריד

Jer 46:28

(a)   ADDRESS

      You
      אתה

(b)   ASSURANCE

      fear not
      אל תירא

(c)   ADDRESS

      O Jacob my servant,
      עבדי יעקב

(d)   ORACULAR FORMULA

      says the LORD,
      נאם יהוה

(e)   BASIS OF ASSURANCE

      for I am with you.
      כי אתך אני

(f)   PROMISE

> I will make a full end of all the nations
> to which I have driven you,
> but of you I will not make a full end.
> I will chasten you in just measure,
> and I will by no means leave you unpunished.
>
> כי אעשה כלה בכל הגוים אשר הדחתיך שמה
> ואתך לא אעשה כלה ויסרתיך למשפט ונקה לא אנקך

The content of these two oracles and other peculiarities of their structure conform to the content and use of the War Oracles in Second Isaiah. In 30:10 and 46:27 there are two Assurances standing in poetic parallelism. This same phenomenon occurs in Isa 41:10. In more prosaic texts the Assurance can be expanded with the addition of more than one phrase (e.g., Josh 8:1-2). We have already observed that there is an additional Assurance in 41:28 which makes it easy to read that verse as constituting a separate War Oracle. The "but you" (ואתה), an Address that introduces both texts, is comparable to the ואתה that introduces the War Oracles in Isa 41:8-16. Here the ואתה, as in Isa 41:8-16, introduces a contrast to the preceding material. Interestingly, the pronoun אתה occurs at the beginning of what we considered a separate War Oracle in 46:28 (it is missing in Jer 30:11). This further suggests that Jer 46:27-28 is constructed as two War Oracles. Although the adversative waw occurred in 46:27, in 46:28 the pronoun occurs without the adversative waw. This suggests that the waw is not to be understood as a necessary part of the genre,[2] but as a clue to the *Sitz im Text* of the genre. As with the War Oracles in Second Isaiah, the community is addressed as Jacob/Israel. In 46:28 the community is addressed simply as "my servant Jacob." This second address of the community by name (which is missing in 30:11) is still another indication that 46:27-28 is constructed as two War Oracles. The Basis of Assurance, occurring only once and introduced by כי, contains the motif of Yahweh's presence (את) with the recipient of the oracle. This is a standard formulation. There is no Basis of Assurance in 46:27, which we have analyzed as a separate oracle. However, in that verse (as well as in 30:10) the Promise is introduced with כי and acts as a kind of Basis of Assurance. In Isa 44:1-5 the Promise introduced by כי also acts as a basis for assurance where the Basis of Assurance is missing. Our analysis of the Promise in 30:11 begins with an infinitive, להושיעך. This infinitive is missing in 46:28. We have noted that in some instances of the genre the infinitive follows a Basis of Assurance, as it does in 30:11, and functions as a Promise (see Jer 1:8). Apart from the infinitive construction, the Promises are formulated in the first person. In 30:10 and 46:27 the Promise parallels Isa 43:1-7 and 44:1-5 in promising the rescue of the offspring (זרע). The Promise in 30:11 and 46:28 indicates that although Yahweh will not make a full end of his people, he will punish them. This motif is not found in the Promise of War Oracles in Second Isaiah; however, in Second Isaiah the War Oracles function in their context to promise salvation to the people after they have already been punished by Yahweh (Isa 40:1-2). The Oracular Formula occurs throughout the Oracles, as is common in War Oracles where the deity, as the source of the oracle, is often identified. All these observations indicate, then, that the two War Oracles in Jer 30:10-11 and 46:27-28 are closely related to the War Oracles in Second Isaiah.

We turn now to a consideration of the *Sitz im Text* of these oracles. Chapter 46 is composed of oracles of Yahweh against Egypt, and military imagery dominates the chapter. Vss. 3-12 concern the defeat of the mighty Egyptian army by Nebuchadrezzar (cf. vs.2). These verses are followed by a poem (vss. 14-24) depicting the terror of Egypt aroused by the approach of the mighty Nebuchadrezzar (cf. vs. 13). A prose section (vss. 25-26) indicates that Yahweh's support of Nebuchadrezzar was responsible for Egypt's defeat. Vs. 26 uses language similar to that we encountered in the Deuteronomic History where Yahweh assured warriors that he had delivered the enemy into their hand. Yahweh says concerning Egypt,

> "Behold, I am bringing punishment upon Amon of Thebes, and Pharoah, and Egypt, and her gods and her kings, upon Pharoah and those who trust in him. I will deliver them into the hand (נתתים ביד) of those who seek their life, into the hand of Nebuchadrezzar king of Babylon and his officers. Afterward Egypt shall be inhabited as in the days of old," says the LORD.

—Jer 46:25b-26

The War Oracles in vss. 27-28, introduced by ואתה ("but you"), as in Isa 41:8-16, stand in contrast to the preceding story of defeat. In the War Oracles Yahweh contrasts his rescue of his people Jacob/Israel from the hand of the enemy with the defeat of Egypt at the hands of Nebuchadrezzar. This *Sitz im Text* is like that in Isa 41 where the War Oracles (Isa 41:8-16) introduced with ואתה announce Yahweh's deliverance of Jacob/Israel from the enemy. This deliverance is contrasted to the impending defeat of the nations in terror at the approach of the conqueror (Isa 41:5-7), a foreigner through whom Yahweh is working to achieve his ends (Isa 41:2-4). Whether or not Jer 46:27-28 was originally composed for this chapter or is part of a collection, the important thing to notice is that the genre, the War Oracle, is appropriately used in this *Sitz im Text*, which is concerned with Yahweh's military defeat of the Egyptians through Nebuchadrezzar, a foreigner. In contrast to the terror of the Egyptians at the advance of Nebuchadrezzar, is the comfort offered by Yahweh to Jacob/Israel with War Oracles promising the ultimate restoration of his offspring.

The *Sitz im Text* of Jer 30:10-11 is considerably different than that of 46:27-28; yet we would argue that the occurrence of the War Oracle in this setting is also understandable. The War Oracle is not accidental, and the implications of the genre are not ignored. Jer 30 shows signs of being well constructed poetry in which the War Oracle has an appropriate expressive function, as was the case in Jer 46 and in Second Isaiah.

There is some indication, however, that the unit immediately preceding the War Oracle (30:8-9) was a later insertion that interrupts the flow of the poetry of the chapter. Other commentators have noted the prosaic character of 30:8-9 and have suggested that it is a later interpolation into the poetry of the chapter.[3] Our form critical observations suggest an additional reason for seeing 30:8-9 as secondary. The War Oracle in 30:10-11 is quite similar to the War Oracles in Second Isaiah where the genre, originally used to address a king, has been appropriated to address the exilic community, Jacob/Israel.

The community assumes the role of the king in the restoration. In Jer 30:8-9, however, the promise for the liberated people is the restoration of the Davidic king (vs. 9). Such an insertion could only have been made at a time when the purpose of the War Oracle—to address the community as king—was not known.

If Jer 30:8-9 is understood as a later insertion, then the War Oracle can be seen to relate directly to the unit preceding it. Jer 30:5-7 describes the panic of Jacob aroused by the coming judgment of Yahweh. "That day" will be a day of great distress for Jacob (30:7). The War Oracle with its opening "but you" introduces a contrast to the panic of Jacob. The War Oracle promises the deliverance of the offspring of Jacob/Israel. It also promises that, although Yahweh will make a full end of the nations, he will not make a full end of Jacob/Israel. The oracle does say, however, that Jacob/Israel will be punished, and it is this motif that is picked up in the unit that follows the War Oracle. Yahweh has punished his people by turning against them like an enemy or a foe.

> All your lovers have forgotten you;
>> they care nothing for you;
> for I have dealt you the blow of an enemy (אויב)
>> the punishment of a merciless foe (אכזרי),
> because your guilt is great,
>> because your sins are flagrant.

—Jer 30:14

Nevertheless, Yahweh will fight on Israel's behalf and see to it that her enemies are destroyed,

> Therefore all who devour you shall be devoured,
>> and all your foes (צריך), every one of them shall go
>>> into captivity;
>> those who despoil you shall become a spoil,
>> and all who prey on you I shall make a prey.

—Jer 30:16

Although Yahweh had treated his people as an enemy, he now says that he will defeat his people's enemies. This unit, then, explains why Yahweh uses a War Oracle; it highlights the reversal that Yahweh will effect: delivering from their enemies the people who were his own enemy. The War Oracle here, like the War Oracle in Isa 43:1-7 and 44:1-5, is used to promise the people deliverance *from* rather than deliverance *to* their enemies. Yahweh will fight for his people as he fights for a king.

These "fear not" oracles in Jeremiah, then, have affinities with the form, function and content of "fear not" oracles in Second Isaiah.[4] As in Second Isaiah, two oracles are joined, although in 30:10-11 the absence of a second Assurance makes it somewhat problematic to analyze the unit as two seperate oracles. In both contexts in Jeremiah the oracles are related to their context by the opening words (ואתה) "but you," as in Isa 41:8-16. Furthermore, their function in their present *Sitz im Text* bears similarities to the function of the oracles in Second Isaiah, where the community Jacob/Israel is comforted by Yahweh with War Oracles (Isa 41:8-16) that contrast Israel's security with the terror of the nations (Isa 41:5-7) at the advance of a foreign conqueror, Cyrus, through whom Yahweh is fighting to deliver his people (41:1-4). In Jer 46 War Oracles (46:27-28) provide the community Jacob/Israel with comfort that contrasts with the terror of the Egyptians (Jer 46:3-24) at the advance of a foreign conqueror Nebuchadrezzar through whom Yahweh is fighting (46:25-26). The "fear not" oracles in

Jer. 30:10-11 functionally parallel the "fear not" oracles in Isa 43:1-7 and 44:1-5. In all three cases the War Oracles contrast Yahweh's promised deliverance of his people with his former warring judgment against them.

The oracles in Jer 30:10-11 and 46:27-28, like the "fear not" oracles in Isa 43:1-7 and 44:1-5, contain Promises rather than Orders and announce that Yahweh will deliver the "offspring" (זרע) of the community. This reference to the rescue of the "offspring" links the oracles in Jeremiah to patriarchal traditions. It appears that Jeremiah intends to address the community as king because the structure of the genre (without an Object of Fear and with Promises) follows the conventions of the genre when it is used in royal contexts.

Zeph 3:16-18a

This "fear not" oracle is frequently understood as a post-exilic oracle influenced by Second Isaiah and added to the genuine sayings of Zephaniah.[5] Although we are not interested here in placing this passage in the editorial history of the book, we will argue that as a War Oracle it sits comfortably in its present *Sitz im Text* and that its form and function have affinities with the form and function of the "fear not" texts in Second Isaiah. As in Second Isaiah, the structure of the War Oracle is characteristic of the genre as used to address a king; and as in Second Isaiah, the War Oracle functions in a context where the community (Zion/Jerusalem)[6] has a royal role of praising the victory of Yahweh, a warrior king who will restore the scattered community and give it renown in the world of nations.

The structure of this War Oracle can be outlined as follows:

(a)   ASSURANCE

      Do not fear,
      אל תיראי

(b)   ADDRESS

      O Zion;
      ציון

(c)   ASSURANCE

      let not your hands grow weak.
      אל ירפו ידיך

(d)   BASIS OF ASSURANCE

> The LORD, your God, is in your midst,
> a warrior who gives victory;
>
> יהוה אלהיך בקרבך גבור יושיע

(e)   PROMISE

> he will rejoice over you with gladness,
> he will renew you in his love;
> he will exult over you with loud singing
> as on the day of a festival.
>
> ישיש עליך בשמחה יחריש באהבתו
> יגיל עליך ברנה נוגי ממועד

As the outline indicates, this War Oracle is structured like those used to address a king, i.e., it lacks an Object of Fear and contains a Promise rather than Orders. Some of the elements are distinctively formed. We have not encountered the phrase, אל ירפו ידיך, as an Assurance before. The Basis of Assurance here is not introduced with כי although the motif of Yahweh being "in your midst" as a "warrior" parallels the often recurring theme that Yahweh as warrior is with the recipient of the oracle. The Basis of Assurance is in the third person, as is the Promise. Both of these elements are usually in the first person. This change in person can be explained by the fact that the oracle is a report of what will be said to Israel "on that day" and not an actual oracle of Yahweh addressed to Israel.

We turn now to consider the *Sitz im Text* of this oracle in Zeph 3. The chapter begins by pronouncing woe on the city with neither accepts correction nor trusts in Yahweh (3:1-2). The problem lies with the leaders of the city—the officials, judges, prophets, and priests, all of whom are corrupt (3:3-5). Because Yahweh had destroyed other nations, the city should have learned from the devastating power of Yahweh that lays nations in ruins. But the city did not learn and became even more corrupt,

> I have cut off nations;
>   their battlements are in ruins;
> I have laid waste their streets
>   so that none walks in them;
> their cities have been made desolate,
>   without a man, without an
>   inhabitant.
> I said, "Surely she will fear me,

> she will accept correction;
> she will not lose sight
> of all that I have enjoined upon
>   her."
> But all the more they were eager
> to make all their deeds corrupt.

—Zeph 3:6-7

Because of the corruption of the city Yahweh therefore will pour out his indignation on all the nations (3:8) so that they will serve him with a single speech (3:9-10). The leaders of the city will be destroyed ("the proudly exultant ones"), and only a "people lowly and humble" will be left in the midst of the city (3:11-13).

It is significant to observe that this unit (3:1-13) does not mention the king in the list of corrupt officials. Nor does it mention the restoration of kingship as an important office for an individual in the new community.[8] Only a small and humble remnant will be left in the city. Taking our cues from Second Isaiah we can infer that the remnant of the community described in Zephaniah is king. Implicit in the "fear not" oracle (Zeph 3:16-18a) is the idea that, as in Second Isaiah, the office of kingship is assumed by the community (Zion/Jerusalem). This royal community, ironically comprising the low and humble, will replace the corrupt leaders in the envisaged future.

The immediate context (Zeph 3:14-20) in which the "fear not" oracle (Zeph 3:16-18a) occurs, bears out this inference that the community is king. The survivors of Yahweh's judgment, "a people humble and lowly" (Zeph 3: 11-13), are given a Directive in Zeph 3:14-15, the unit that immediately precedes the War Oracle.

> Sing aloud, O daughter of Zion;
>   shout, O Israel!
> Rejoice and exult with all your heart,
>   O daughter of Jerusalem!
> The LORD has taken away the
>   judgments against you,
>   he has cast out your enemies.
> The King of Israel, the LORD, is
>   in your midst;
>   you shall fear evil no more.

This Directive is like the one given to Zion/Jerusalem in the first chapter of Second Isaiah.

Get you up to a high mountain,
   O Zion, herald of good tidings;
lift up your voice with strength,
   O Jerusalem, herald of good
     tidings,
    lift it up, fear not;
say to the cities of Judah,
   "Behold your God!"
Behold, the Lord GOD comes with
    might,
   and his arm rules for him;
behold, his reward is with him,
   and his recompense before him.
He will feed his flock like a
    shepherd,
   he will gather the lambs in his
    arms,
he will carry them in his bosom,
   and gently lead those that are with
    young.

—Isa 40:9-11

In both Directives Zion/Jerusalem[9] is commanded to celebrate the victory of Yahweh. The vocation of the community in Zephaniah, then, is like the vocation of the royal community in Second Isaiah.[10] Furthermore, the specific reasons for the festive praise in Zephaniah are similar to those in Second Isaiah. In Zephaniah, Zion/Jerusalem is to praise Yahweh because (1) her judgments (משפטים) have been taken away, (2) her enemies (איביך) have been cast out, and (3) Yahweh is in her midst as a warrior. Likewise in Second Isaiah, Zion/Jerusalem is to praise Yahweh because (1) she has paid double for all her sins (חטאתיה, Isa 40:2), (2) her warfare (צבאה) has ended (Isa 40:2), and (3) Yahweh as victorious warrior is present or will be present with his people (Isa 40:3-5 and 40:10).

War Oracles in Second Isaiah (41:8-16; 43:1-7 and 44:1-5) come after the initial Directive and assure the royal community in its vocation of praising the divine warrior, a vocation associated with kingship. The War Oracle in Zephaniah, which immediately follows the Directive, functions in the same way: to assure the community in its celebration of the victory of the warrior Yahweh—a royal vocation.

The motif of Yahweh as a warrior who fights for royalty, in this case a royal community of humble survivors, is evident in the War Oracle itself. The Basis of Assurance states that Yahweh, "the warrior who gives victory," is in the midst of his people. That the royal community is the center of his concern is evident in the promise proclaiming that Yahweh will sing in festive exultation of the people. This echoes the preceding Directive exhorting the community to make festive shouts of praise to Yahweh.

There is one other link between the War Oracle and its context in Zephaniah and the War Oracles in Second Isaiah. The unit that follows the War Oracle in Zephaniah (Zeph 3:18b-20) adds a further Promise of Yahweh. This Promise in the first person is more typical than the third person Promise of the War Oracle proper. Significantly, the themes developed in this Promise are similar to the themes in the Promises of the War Oracles in Isa 43:1-7 and 44:1-5. In Zephaniah it is promised that Yahweh will gather the oppressed (including the lame and the outcast) and give them renown, i.e., a name (שם) in all the earth. Likewise in Isa 43:1-7 and 44:1-5 the community is promised that the offspring of the community will be gathered and renowned (cf. 43:7 and 44:5).

The discussion of the "fear not" oracle and its *Sitz im Text* in Zephaniah can be summarized as follows. Structurally, the oracle is similar to the genre when it is used to address a king, i.e., the missing Object of Fear is characteristic, as is the use of a Promise. Furthermore, the oracle concerns the action of the deity as warrior. The *Sitz im Text* stresses the vocation of the community as one of praising the warrior Yahweh; such a vocation is typical of royalty. That Zion/Jerusalem is a royal community makes sense when the larger context of Zeph 3 is considered. The judgment of Yahweh will remove the corrupt leaders of the city so that only a lowly and humble people will survive. It is this community that will be king and become renowned in all the earth. While it is difficult to argue for direct connections between Zephaniah and Second Isaiah in the use of the War Oracle, the genre functions in a similar way in both texts. It is used to address the community, whose role is the royal vocation of praising Yahweh, and to promise that Yahweh's victory as warrior will result in the restoration of the community.

Isa 10:24-27

Isaiah 10 is understood by critics to be a collection of genuine sayings of Isaiah and units added by later editors; the "fear not" oracle (Isa 10: 24-27) is generally considered to be one of the later interpolations.[12] We are not interested, however, in tracing the editorial history of this prophetic book but in looking at the chapter in its final form. Our thesis is that in Isa 10 the "fear not" oracle is a War Oracle and that its *Sitz im Text* is similar to the textual settings in Isa 41 and Jer 46.

The structure of this "fear not" oracle clearly identifies it as a War Oracle:

(a) PROPHETIC MESSENGER FORMULA

> Therefore thus says the Lord, the LORD of hosts:
> לכן כה אמר אדני יהוה צבאות

(b) ASSURANCE

> Be not afraid,
> אל תירא

(c) ADDRESS

> O my people who dwell in Zion,
> עמי ישב ציון

(d) OBJECT OF FEAR

> of the Assyrians when they smite with the rod and lift up their staff against you as the Egyptians did.
> מאשור בשבט יככה ומטהו ישא עליך בדרך מצרים

(e) BASIS OF ASSURANCE

> For in a very little while my indignation will come to an end, and my anger will be directed to their destruction.
> כי עוד מעט מזער וכלה זעם ואפי על תבליתם

(f) PROMISE

> And the LORD of hosts will wield against them a scourge, as when he smote Midian at the rock of Oreb; and his rod will be over the sea, and he will lift it as he did in Egypt. And in that day his burden will depart from your shoulder, and his yoke will be destroyed from your neck.
> ועורר עליו יהוה צבאות שוט כמכת מדין בצור עורב ומטהו
> על הים ונשאו בדרך מצרים והיה ביום ההוא יסור סבלו מעל
> שכמך ועלו מעל צוארך וחבל על מפני שמן

This text manifests the structure of the conventional War Oracle. The Assurance is the expected אל תירא ; the Basis of Assurance is introduced by כי and the Object of Fear by מן. The Oracle contains a Promise and like Zeph 3:16-17 is formulated in the third person. Delivered by a prophet, the oracle uses the prophetic messenger formula. In structure, then, this oracle is closely related to the oracles Isaiah delivered to Ahaz (Isa 7:4-9) and to Hezekiah (Isa 36:6-7), War Oracles used to comfort kings faced with military invasion. Here, however, the oracle is not delivered to a king but, as in the later texts in Second Isaiah, Jeremiah and Zephaniah, is addressed to the community identified in Isa 10: 24-27 as "my people who dwell in Zion."

It will be helpful to examine the larger context, beginning in Isa 9, to understand the related concepts of king and community. After the unit on the future ideal king (9:2-7), the chapter turns to a description of the coming judgment of Yahweh against his people (9:8-10:47). This judgment will come because the leadership of the community has failed,

> The people did not turn to him who
>   smote them,
>   nor seek the LORD of hosts.
> So the LORD cut off from Israel
>   head and tail,
>   palm branch and reed in one day —
> the elder and honored man is the
>   head,
>   and the prophet who teaches lies
>   is the tail;
> for those who lead this people lead
>   them astray,
>   and those who are led by them
>   are swallowed up.

—Isa 9:13-16

The judgment of Yahweh is described as a "burning" judgment. The next unit (10:5-11) makes it clear that this judgment of Yahweh will be carried out through Assyria, described as "the rod of my anger" (vs. 5) who arrogantly boasts, "Are not my commanders all kings?" (vs.8). The implication of this unit is that the warring activity is conducted through kings—in this case a foreign king who will destroy Jerusalem. At this point the chapter moves beyond the envisaged judgment of Yahweh's people to the period beyond the judgment. In 10:12-19 the judgment of Yahweh is directed against Assyria, the rod of his anger, because Assyria in its pride does not know that Yahweh is the source of its power to wage war successfully. The "burning" anger of Yahweh will now be turned against Assyria and its warriors (vs.16ff). The text next moves to the survivors among Yahweh's people (10:20-23). Even though the people are like "the sand of the sea"—an allusion to the promise of posterity to the patriarchs (cf. Gen 22:7; Isa 48:19)—only a remnant will return (vs. 22). It is to this remnant, to the survivors, that Yahweh addresses the War Oracle in 10:24-27c. Here the people who dwell in Zion are not to be afraid of the Assyrians (Object of Fear) who oppressed them as had the Egyptians because (Basis of Assurance) Yahweh's anger against his people will come to an end and will be directed against the Assyrians, so that the community will be delivered from the oppressor just as Israel had been delivered from the Egyptians. The War Oracle is followed by a description of the advance of the Assyrians which will be cut down by Yahweh as a forest is hewn down (10:27d-34). Another poem on the future ideal king (11:1-9) forms an inclusion with 9:2-7.

The context of Isa 10:24-27, then, is bracketed by poems in chapters 9 and 11 concerning the future ideal king. Who is this ideal king? Our identification of Isa 10:24-27 as a War Oracle addressed to "the people of Zion" suggests that the community is king.

The *Sitz im Text* of the Oracle, the material beginning and ending with these two poems on ideal kingship, has distinct parallels to those late "fear not" texts in Second Isaiah, Jeremiah and Zephaniah where the community is comforted as a king facing the prospect of war.

Like the War Oracle and its context in Zeph 3, the oracle here is addressed to the community surviving the judgment of Yahweh, a judgment which results from the corruption and perversion of the leaders of the community. While the leaders of the community have failed, Yahweh will fight for the future of the royal community, the remnant who survive his judgment.

The *Sitz im Text* of this oracle is also similar to the textual settings of the oracles in Jer 30, Isa 43 and Isa 44: while Yahweh does turn against his people in war, he will fight again for his people so that there will be future offspring. In Isa 10 the hope inherent in the return of the remnant is linked to the past promise of posterity through the patriarchal allusion to "the sand of the sea" in vs. 22, which serves the double purpose of (1) accentuating the enormity of the judgment by comparing the small remnant to the vast population which had been the fulfillment of past promise and of (2) intensifying the hope by evoking an image of a great population that will emerge from a remnant.

Finally, the *Sitz im Text* of this "fear not" oracle also has striking affinities with the *Sitz im Text* of the oracles in Isa 41 and Jer 46. In both those texts it is stated that Yahweh is fighting in the world of nations through a foreign king—Cyrus in Isa 41 and Nebuchadrezzar in Jer 46. In both places, however, the royal community is comforted with War Oracles which assure Israel that Yahweh is fighting on their behalf for their deliverance. The royal community of Yahweh does not need to fight. Similarly here Yahweh is fighting through a foreign power Assyria. His own kings—in this case the royal community—do not need to fight; it is Yahweh who is fighting for them.

In summary, then, both the structure and setting of the "fear not" oracle in Isa 10 are like those of other late "fear not" texts in Second Isaiah, Jeremiah and Zephaniah. Yahweh comforts a royal community that, though small in number, will have a future posterity. This small and powerless community need not fight: Yahweh's kings do not fight. Yahweh fights through foreign kings not only against his people but ultimately for his people. Like kings (e.g., Ps 89:37-38), the community will have offspring that will endure forever. The roots of this promise, as we will see in the next chapter, are in the promise to the royal father of Israel, Abraham.[13]

CHAPTER VII

THE PATRIARCHAL PROMISE AND THE WAGING OF PEACE

Introduction

It has been argued in the last two chapters that War Oracles were used in exilic and post-exilic texts to address the community as king. In all these texts the hope of the community in the victory of Yahweh is grounded in the promise to the patriarchs of a future posterity. The identity of this royal community, therefore, is traced to its origins in the patriarchs, most notably Abraham. This identification is made explicit in Second Isaiah in a War Oracle where Jacob/Israel is specifically called the offspring of Abraham (Isa 41:8, cf. 2 Chr 20:7).

In this chapter we will argue that in the book of Genesis, which tells the story of Jacob/Israel's origins, the patriarchs are addressed with royal War Oracles promising them a future posterity. The story of Israel's origins parallels the prophetic hope. Yahweh fights for his community to insure it a future. Jacob/Israel, like a king, is not to be actively engaged in battle; Yahweh will fight for him.

In Genesis, as in the exilic and post-exilic texts (especially Second Isaiah), Abraham is the paradigmatic warrior-king for whom Yahweh fights. Like Abraham, the ideal warrior-king, Jacob/Israel should play a passive role in warfare for it is Yahweh who gives the victory.

Gen 15:1b: The Structure

The picture of Abraham as the model warrior for the community becomes apparent when Gen 15:1b is understood as a War Oracle in its *Sitz im Text*, Gen 14 and 15. Our discussion of this pericope will begin with a consideration of its structure, which can be outlined as follows:

(a) ASSURANCE

Fear not,
אל תירא

(b) ADDRESS

Abram,
אברם

124

(c)   BASIS OF ASSURANCE

I am your shield;

אנכי מגן לך

(d)   PROMISE

your reward shall be very great.

שכרך הרבה מאד

The structure of this oracle is like that of War Oracles used to address a king. There is a Promise rather than Orders. Also, the Address is typical not only of extra-biblical royal War Oracles but also of oracles used to address the community as king, as, for example, in Second Isaiah. The Basis of Assurance, normally introduced by כי, is sometimes missing (cf. Isa 41:14) as it is here. When an oracle is spoken directly by Yahweh, the Promise is usually in the first person. Here Yahweh speaks in the first person in the Basis of Assurance and promises to make Abraham's reward great. Interestingly, the Samaritan Pentateuch has the first person singular imperfect ארבה for the MT's infinitive absolute הרבה.[1]

Gen 15:1b: *Other Connotations of Royalty and War*

The vocabulary of this oracle also links it with royalty and war. In the Basis of Assurance, Yahweh identifies himself as the shield (מגן) of Abraham. Other scholars have, of course, recognized the military connotations of this term. For example O. Kaiser comments,

> Die Selbsprädikation der Gottheit "Ich bin dein Schild." . . . weist
> zunächst ganz allgemein in den Raum der Kriegsideologie.[2]

In the Hebrew Scriptures the deity is sometimes designated as a "shield" (מגן), especially in connection with some military undertaking or war setting. In the conclusion to the Blessing of Moses (Deut 33:26-29), for example, Yahweh is portrayed as a divine warrior,[3] and is described there as "the shield of your (Israel's) help and the sword of your triumph" (מגן עזרך ואשר חרב גאותך, vs. 29b). Other psalms portray the deity as the shield of the people in situations of war. For example, Ps 33 is a hymn to Yahweh celebrating his creation and sovereignty in history. God is pictured in vss. 13-17 as being enthroned in heaven and looking down from heaven on the inhabitants of the earth. A contrast is suggested between Yahweh's power and earthly powers of war.

A king (המלך) is not saved by his great army (ברב חיל)

   a warrior (גבור) is not delivered by his great strength.

The war horse (הסוס) is a vain hope for victory,

   and by its great might it cannot save.

—Ps 33:16-17

Rather than in these earthly powers of military might the Psalmist places his hope in Yahweh whom he calls "our shield" (מגננו), vs. 20. Describing God as shield, then, signifies the deity's power in war.[4] However, the shield imagery may also be used, as it is in a number of psalms, to suggest the close relationship between god and the king. Just as the king, the anointed (משיח), is often called the מגן and protector of the people (Pss 84:10 and 89:19), so the deity is often designated as the shield and protector of the king, in face of enemies and in times of battle. The psalm found in 2 Sam 22 (virtually the same as Ps 18) is a king's psalm of thanksgiving to Yahweh for victory in a battle described in vss. 32-43. In this psalm the king in vs. 3 refers to the deity as "my shield" (מגני); in vs. 31 he says "he (Yahweh) is a shield for all those who take refuge in him" (מגן הוא לכל החסים בו); and in vs. 36 he says to the deity, "Thou hast given me the shield of thy salvation" (ותתן לי מגן ישעך). Likewise in Ps 144, a royal lament in which the king prays for victory in battle (vss. 9-10), the deity readying the king for war (vs. 1) is designated as the shield of the king,

> my rock and my fortress,
> > my stronghold and my deliverer,
> my shield (מגני) and he in whom
> > I take refuge
> who subdues the people under him.

Ps 144:2

In addition to these biblical texts which portray the deity as the shield of the king,[5] there is a War Oracle addressed to Esarhaddon in which the deity describes herself as the king's shield,

O Esarhaddon, in Arbela I am your good shield.[6]

In short, then, the associations of the word "shield" with war and kingship in Gen 15:1b reinforce our understanding of the text as a royal War Oracle.[7]

The word שכר ("reward") that occurs in the Promise also has military connotations; it can refer to the "booty" of the victor in war.[8] שכר has this meaning, for example, in Ezek 29:19 in an oracle that Yahweh speaks concerning Nebuchadrezzar:

> Behold, I will give the land of Egypt to Nebuchadrezzar king of
> Babylon; and he shall carry off its wealth and despoil it and plunder
> it; and it shall be the wages (שכר) for his army.

In Isa 40:10 Yahweh, the divine warrior, is pictured as bringing the booty (שכל) from his

victory with him (cf. Isa 62:11). The word שכר, then, which can refer to the booty or

spoils of war, is appropriate to the War Oracle in Gen 15:1b.

Gen 15:1b: Its Sitz im Text

Both the structure and content of Gen 15:1b suggest that we are dealing with a royal

War Oracle. The present literary context also suggest that 15:1b is a royal War Oracle.

It appropriately follows the story of Gen 14 where Abraham is—uniquely for the book of

Genesis—portrayed as an active warrior. But why would Yahweh address Abraham as a

warrior-king after the war is over? The answer to that question is a clue to the meaning

of the *Sitz im Text* of Gen 15:1b and is prompted by our understanding of the way the

genre functions in Second Isaiah. Just as Yahweh in Second Isaiah addresses Jacob/Israel

with War Oracles when the community's warfare has ended, so here Yahweh addresses

Abraham after his warfare is over. This royal ancestor Abraham, like the royal

community Jacob/Israel, does not need to fight. Yahweh will fight for him and give him

the victory. In Gen 15, as in Second Isaiah, the booty of the war Yahweh fights is the

"offspring" (זרע) of the community.

The first time War Oracles occur in Second Isaiah, Yahweh addresses the community

as the "offspring of Abraham, my friend" (Isa 41:8). In this Genesis story of Israel's

origins Yahweh addresses the ancestor directly to say that Yahweh's people do not need

to fight in order to survive; Yahweh will fight for them. Nowhere in Gen 14 is Abraham

given orders to fight. He conducts the warfare on his own initiative. The point of the

War Oracle is that Abraham, like a king, should play a more passive role. It is Yahweh

who will fight for him to insure the survival of the community.

Having spoken generally about the *Sitz im Text* of Gen 15:1b, we will now turn to a

more specific discussion of the relation of the War Oracle in Gen 15:1b to the preceding

account of the warrior Abraham in Gen 14. The War Oracle is linked to the preceding

text (Gen 14) with the words, "After these things the word of Yahweh came to Abram in

a vision." Source critics have sometimes argued that the phrase, "after these things"

(אחר הדברים האלה) is "a very indefinite temporal connection with no indication whatever that any specific prior events are related to what follows."[9] Such a conclusion, however, is forced on the scholar whose analysis of the text to identify underlying sources strips the phrase from its literary context. Rather than being "a very indefinite temporal connection," the phrase is a key to understanding the *Sitz im Text* of the War Oracle. The phrase signals a change in the situation. "After these things," after the war which Abram fights on his own initiative, Yahweh now speaks to Abram as he would speak to a king about his non-combatant role in warfare. Abram's active participation in war has come to an end, for Yahweh now promises Abram with a War Oracle that he will fight for Abram and give him booty. Abram does not need to fight. Indeed, "after these things," neither Abram nor his descendants are presented in the rest of the book of Genesis as warriors in the conventional sense.

The phrase "the word of the LORD came to . . ." (. . .היה דבר יהוה אל) has been recognized by scholars as a technical formula for reporting a speech to a prophet.[10] A prophetic link makes sense here because the War Oracle addressed to kings is spoken in the Hebrew Scriptures by prophets. Jeremiah's autobiographical account of the War Oracle addressed to him as a prophetic warrior is preceded by a similar phrase, "now the word of the LORD came to me" (ויהי דבר יהוה אלי), Jer 1:4. That this word, this War Oracle, came to Abram "in a vision" (במחזה)[11] is also consistent with our understanding of the communication of War Oracles. Throughout the study we have emphasized the importance of vision, which is usually concerned with the Basis of Assurance (see, e.g., Josh 8:1-2 and Jer 1). Also we noted that a War Oracle was communicated to Ashurbanipal in an oracular dream.[12]

The phrase, "after these things the word of the LORD came to Abram in a vision" (Gen 15:1a), then, serves as a transition from the active warfare of Abram in Gen 14 to his regal position as non-combatant in Gen 15:1b. Other rhetorical links need to be pointed out between Gen 14 and Gen 15:1b, but before considering these rhetorical relationships a few words need to be said about the setting of Gen 14 in general.

Gen 14 concerns an alliance of four kings who eventually became a threat to Abram when they take his nephew Lot as a hostage. This alliance of kings is reminiscent of the alliances of kings who threatened Ahaz, Zakir and Ashurbanipal. Abram is not presented as a king here, however, and what is threatened is not his kingship but the safety of the exiled offspring of the family. The offspring are not Abram's direct descendants but his brother's offspring. Abram takes the initiative and wins the battle. When he returns with the booty, two kings come out to meet him—the formerly defeated king of Sodom and Melchizedek, the king of Salem, the priest of God Most High. Melchizedek blesses Abram by God Most High. The king of Sodom, apparently assuming the booty to be his, offers all of it, except the persons, to Abram. The blessing of Melchizedek and the transaction with the king of Sodom throw further light on the *Sitz im Text* of the War Oracle in Gen 15:1b.

Melchizedek, the king of Salem and the priest of God Most High, blessed Abram as ⊃llows:

> Blessed be Abram by God Most High,
>   Maker of heaven and earth;
> and blessed be God Most High,
>   who has delivered (מגן) your
>   enemies (צריך) into your hand (בידך).

—Gen 14:19-20

The important thing to notice about this blessing is that Melchizedek, after blessing Abram, blesses God Most High who is described as being responsible for Abram's victory. Melchizedek's understanding that the deity had given Abram the victory is consistent with the notion that Yahweh gave victory to his people by fighting through foreign warriors (e.g., Cyrus in Isa 41; Nebuchadrezzar in Jer 46 and Assyria in Isa 10). It appears here that the king, Melchizedek, who does not fight but plays a passive role in the battle which led to victory, is blessing the active warrior Abram.

When Melchizedek says in the blessing that it was God Most High "who delivered your enemies into your hand" (אשר מגן צריך בידך), he is using a phrase that echoes the Basis of Assurance in War Oracles used to address active warriors in the Deuteronomic History, "I have given . . . into your hands" (נתתי...בידך). But why would the rare word מגן be used in Melchizedek's blessing rather than the more common and conventional נתנו?[13] It is used to link rhetorically Melchizedek's blessing with the Basis of Assurance in the War Oracle spoken to Abram in Gen 15:1b.[14] Yahweh the "shield" (מגן) of Abram in Gen 15:1b is God Most High, who Melchizedek claimed, had "delivered" or "given" (מגן) Abram's enemies into his hand, Gen 14:20. This rhetorical connection between the blessing of Melchizedek and the War Oracle of Yahweh makes it clear that it is Yahweh, the shield, who has given Abram the victory.

This association of Yahweh with God Most High is made explicit in Abram's response to the king of Sodom in their transaction regarding the sharing of the booty. The king of Sodom says that Abram should give him the persons (הנפש), presumably those who were taken hostage by enemy as was Lot, but that Abram should keep the goods or the booty (הרכש). Abram refuses to take the booty because he says he had made a vow with Yahweh God Most High that he would not take anything lest the king of Sodom would say that he had made Abram rich; Abram would take nothing except what the young men had eaten and the share of those men who had gone with him. Here Abram identifies Yahweh as God Most High. It was Yahweh who had given Abram the victory.

The king of Sodom who, although involved in an earlier battle in which he was defeated, was not an active participant in the battle won by the foreign warrior, Abram, laid claim to the booty. He offered the booty to Abram,[15] but Abram was not dependent on the king of Sodom for spoils of war. The refusal of Abram to accept the "booty" (רכש) from the king of Sodom has connections with the War Oracle in Gen 15:1b. Abram is promised in the War Oracle that Yahweh will make his "booty" (שכר) great.

Before moving on it will be helpful to draw together the points made about Gen 14 and its relationship to the War Oracle in Gen 15:1b. In Gen 14 Abram is an active warrior fighting for others. He fights in a battle for the kings of Sodom and Salem to liberate Lot his nephew. While he does this on his own initiative, it becomes clear that Yahweh has given him the victory; Yahweh is identified as God Most High. "After these things," Yahweh speaks a War Oracle to Abram. This War Oracle with its royal connotations makes it clear that Yahweh will now fight for Abram; the one who had himself fought for kings will now assume the non-combatant role of a king. Abram's warfare is over; Abram the warrior has become "king," and Yahweh will fight for him.

When it is seen that Abram is addressed by Yahweh as Yahweh would address a king, Abram's lament in 15:2-3 becomes clear.[16] Abram is lamenting the fact that the booty of a king is not appropriate because he is childless. Without offspring how can Abram's future be secured? The heir of his house is a slave, Eliezer. In response to Abram's lament Yahweh states what Abram's reward will be. Abram will have a son who will be his heir (vs. 4)[17] and his descendants (זרע) will be like the stars of the heavens (vs. 5). The promise given to Abram, then, is like the promise reiterated to the royal community

Jacob/Israel in War Oracles in Second Isaiah and in other War Oracles in proto-apocalyptic texts. Abram will have a great posterity.

We are told in vs. 6 that Abram "believed" (האמן) and that Yahweh reckoned it to him as righteousness. This response of Abram is also to be understood in relationship to the royal War Oracle. In the War Oracle addressed to Ahaz, in Isa 7:4-9, Ahaz was given conditional orders by Yahweh.

> If you do not believe (תאמינו),
> surely you shall not be
> established (תאמנו).

—Isa 7:9b

While Ahaz did not believe in the oracle of Yahweh that promised him a future, Abraham did. The importance of "believing" in Yahweh who gives War Oracles to royalty was also noted in our discussion of 2 Chr 20. In this chapter a War Oracle (2 Chr 20:15-17) is given in response to Jehoshaphat's prayer to Yahweh (2 Chr 20:6-12) in which he asks for judgment upon an alliance of foreign nations threatening him. In the prayer Jehoshaphat identifies the community as "the descendants of Abraham, your (Yahweh's) friend" (זרע אברהם אהבך). As in Second Isaiah (Isa 41:8), then, the community in the situation of war described in 2 Chr 20 is associated with the patriarch Abraham. Significantly, after the War Oracle, Jehoshaphat gives a Directive to the community, the descendants of Abraham, that is reminiscent of the orders given to Ahaz and a challenge to be like their royal ancestor Abraham,

> Hear me, Judah and inhabitants of Jerusalem! Believe (האמינו) in
> the LORD your God, and you will be established (ותאמנו); believe
> (האמינו) his prophets and you will succeed.

—2 Chr 20:20b

Following the statement concerning Abram's belief in the words of Yahweh (Gen 15:6) is the description of a ceremony in which Yahweh concludes a covenant with Abram. While this covenant has often been linked with the Davidic Covenant and further strengthens our association of Abraham with kingship in Gen 15,[18] it is important here to point out the significance of the promise of descendants that comes in the middle of this ceremony, Gen 15:13-16. These verses represent an additional link between the settings of the War Oracles in Gen 15 and in Second Isaiah and other proto-apocalyptic texts where War Oracles are used to promise the return of the offspring.

Then the LORD said to Abram, "Know of a surety that your
descendants (זרעך) will be sojourners in a land that is not theirs, and
will be slaves there, and they will be oppressed for four hundred
years; but I will bring judgment on the nation which they serve, and
afterwards they shall come out with great possessions. As for
yourself, you shall go to your fathers in peace; you shall be buried in
a good old age. And they shall come back here in the fourth
generation; for the iniquity of the Amorites is not yet complete."

—Gen 15:13-16

As in Second Isaiah and the other proto-apocalyptic texts we have considered, this
promise envisions the enslavement of Abram's offspring in exile and their eventual
restoration.[19]

It is important to observe here also that Abram will die in peace (בשלום). He will
not die the violent death of a warrior but the peaceful death of one for whom Yahweh
fights. Abram will be like Solomon whom Yahweh will grant peace (1 Chr 22:9)[20]

In summary, then, the War Oracle in Gen 15:1b follows the conventions of the War
Oracle used to address a king. The warrior Abraham who fought for kings (Gen 14) is
himself addressed as a king in Gen 15:1b. His active participation in warfare has come to
an end, and he will assume the non-combatant role of a king. As a king he is promised an
heir and a great posterity. Even though his descendants will be enslaved in a foreign
land, Yahweh will bring judgment on the nation which will oppress them, and Yahweh will
deliver the offspring.

The War Oracle and its *Sitz im Text* in this story of Israel's origins has parallels with
the War Oracle and its *Sitz im Text* in the vision of Second Isaiah and other proto-
apocalyptic texts. Abraham is the paradigmatic warrior for the subsequent community
who are his offspring (cf. Isa 41:8 and 2 Chr 20:7). He is also the ideal royal father of the
community for, unlike kings such as Ahaz who put their trust in human powers and who
do not trust in Yahweh as warrior, Abraham believes. It is in this ancestor that the later
community enslaved in exile can hope. They can look forward to the restoration of the
offspring of Abraham, and like Abraham they will live to a "good old age" and die in
peace. Just as Yahweh waged peace for Abraham, he will wage peace for the community
in exile.

Gen 26:24

This "fear not" oracle addressed to Isaac, Abraham's heir, occurs in a context where Abraham's descendant encounters conflict with Abimelech, king of Gerar and his people. It is an example of how Yahweh wages peace for the descendants of Abraham. It also reiterates the promise of a great posterity to Isaac.

The structure of this oracle is as follows:

(a)   SELF-DESIGNATION OF THE DEITY

I am the God of Abraham, your father;
אנכי אלהי אברהם אביך

(b)   ASSURANCE

fear not,
אל תירא

(c)   BASIS OF ASSURANCE

for I am with you,
כי אתך אנכי

(d)   PROMISE

and will bless you and multiply your descendants for my servant Abraham's sake.
וברכתיך והרביתיך את זרעך בעבור אברהם עבדי

The Assurance with אל תירא and the Basis of Assurance introduced by כי and containing the motif of Yahweh's presence with (את) the recipient of the oracle are typical of the language of war. The missing Object of Fear and the occurrence of a Promise in the first person singular are typical of this language when a deity addresses a king with a War Oracle. The Self-Designation of the Deity is not typical of the genre, but it does occur in some extra-biblical oracles (see Appendix II). Here it also identifies Yahweh who delivers the oracle to Isaac as the same deity who delivered the earlier War Oracle to Abram.

What can be said about the *Sitz im Text* of this War Oracle? The first thing to notice is that just as Abram's oracle came to him in a vision so Isaac's oracle comes to him in a vision. It came to him when "Yahweh appeared to him on the same night" (וירא אליו יהוה בלילה ההוא). Once again we are reminded of the War Oracle revealed to Ashurbanipal in an oracular dream.

This oracle appears in a pericope (Gen 26:23-25) in the middle of an account of Isaac's sojourn with Abimelech at Gerar. While it could be argued that the pericope is a later insertion into the text because it interrupts the flow of the narrative,[21] we would argue that the disruptive character of this pericope is a clue to the *Sitz im Text* of the oracle. Before the War Oracle there is a series of conflicts between Isaac and Abimelech and his people. The War Oracle in its present setting assures Isaac that Yahweh is fighting for him to resolve the conflict and to wage peace with Isaac's enemies.

Gen 26 begins with the ominous note that there is a famine in the land which puts the future of Abram's descendant Isaac in jeopardy. At this time Isaac goes to Gerar, to Abimelech, the king of the Philistines (26:1). Yahweh appears to Isaac and gives him an order to stay in the land and not to go down to Egypt. At this time he renews the promise which he made to Abram in Gen 15 that Isaac's descendants would be like the stars of the heaven and that his descendants would be given "all these lands." He also reiterates the promise given to Abraham in Gen 12:1-3 that in Isaac's descendants all the nations will bless themselves because of Abraham who obeyed Yahweh (26:2-5).

At this point in the narrative Isaac knows the promises of Yahweh, but Abimelech and his people, a potential nation to receive blessing through the descendants of Isaac, do not. Because Isaac is afraid (ירא, vs. 7) during his sojourn in Gerar, he pretends that Rebekah is his sister rather than his wife. While this creates conflict with Abimelech, Abimelech orders that neither Isaac nor Rebekah be harmed (26:6-12). When Isaac prospers in Gerar, another conflict ensues with Abimelech who orders him to leave, "Go away from us; for you are much mightier than we" (26:11-17). After Isaac leaves and encamps in the valley of Gerar and begins to dig wells, he encounters conflict with the herdsmen of Gerar. Finally he is able to dig a well without contention, and he attributes his success to Yahweh. In all the conflicts between Isaac and Abimelech and between Isaac and the inhabitants of Gerar, Yahweh protects Isaac and causes him to prosper.

After these episodes of conflict, which are all resolved so that Isaac not only survives but becomes prosperous, the War Oracle is delivered (26:24). The War Oracle functions to make clear to Isaac that Yahweh is fighting for him—waging peace for him, settling the quarrels with his enemies and promising him a future posterity. After the War Oracle, the narrative makes clear that Isaac's conflict (his "warfare") is over. Abimelech the king along with Ahuzzath his advisor and Phicol, the commander of the army, come to make a covenant with Isaac for they see plainly that Yahweh is "with" (עם)

Isaac (26:26-30). That Yahweh had waged peace for Isaac is evident in vs. 30 where it is

stated that Isaac departed "in peace" (בשלום).

Here the War Oracle functions to assure Isaac that Yahweh is fighting for him,

waging peace. The consequence of this action of Yahweh is that Isaac has become a

"witness" to another nation who can see that Yahweh is with Isaac. In recognizing that

Yahweh is with Isaac, Abimelech receives a blessing—he can live in peace with Isaac. In

Second Isaiah Jacob/Israel was to be a witness to the nations of Yahweh's victory; here

Isaac becomes a witness to Abimelech and his people.

Gen 21:17-18

This oracle is addressed to Hagar. As we will see, it is structually somewhat

distinctive and is more like the oracles addressed to Esarhaddon[22] than other War

Oracles in the Hebrew Scriptures. Like the Esarhaddon oracles, it is concerned more

with the general protection of the king (in this case Hagar's son) than with the specific

setting of war. The *Sitz im Text* of the oracle, however, is similar to that of the War

Oracle addressed to Isaac in Gen 26:24, i.e., the oracle occurs, along with an account of

the conflict between Hagar and Sarah, in the midst of an account concerning conflicts

between Abraham and Abimelech. As in Gen 26, after the oracle is spoken, Abimelech

sees that God is with Abraham. On this basis Abraham and Abimelech conclude a

covenant.

The structure of this oracle is as follows:

(a)   DISPUTATION QUESTION

> What troubles you, Hagar?
> מה לך הגר

(b)   ASSURANCE

> Fear not;
> אל תיראי

(c)   BASIS OF ASSURANCE

> for God has heard the voice of the child where he is.
> כי שמע אלהים אל קול הנער באשר הוא שם

(d)   DIRECTIVE

   Arise, lift up the lad, and hold him fast with your hand;

   קומי שאי את הנער והחזיקי את ידך בו

(e)   PROMISE

   for I will make him a great nation.

   כי לגוי גדול אשימנו

This oracle contains many of the elements common to the War Oracle. The Assurance is אל תיראי, the Basis of Assurance is introduced by כי and contains a verb in the perfect tense, and the Promise contains a verb in the first person imperfect tense. The preposition כי sometimes introduces a Promise as it does here (see Isa 44:1-5). The Directive is characteristic of the language of war. However, unlike Directives in offensive situations (cf. Josh 8:1-2), it does not direct Hagar to initiate a war. Nor does it command Hagar to be still (cf. Isa 7:4-9) as do War Oracles addressed to kings. Instead, it commands Hagar to care for her son. The Directive is, therefore, somewhat unusual, as is the Disputation Question. We noted the importance of Disputation Questions in Second Isaiah where we argued that they act as a means of persuasion. We also noted in our discussion of Second Isaiah that the Disputation Question regularly occurs in oracles addressed to Esarhaddon (see Appendix II).

   The structure of this oracle, then, is somewhat distinctive. Like the Esarhaddon oracles, it represents an extension of the use of the War Oracle to refer to the general protection of the king by the deity. This oracle is similar in structure to the one addressed to Esarhaddon in response to the complaint of the king's mother:

(a)   SELF-DESIGNATION OF THE DEITY

   I, the Lady of Arbela, (say) to the king's mother:

(b)   DISPUTATION

   "Because you have complained against me (saying) 'He who is at the right and he who is at the left you hold on your lap, but where is my offspring? You make him run about (unprotected) in the open country!' "

(c)   ADDRESS

   Now, O King,

(d)   ASSURANCE

   fear not!

(e)   BASIS OF ASSURANCE

Yours is the kingship! Yours is the might![23]

In the Assyrian text the deity disputes the complaint of the king's mother that her son was left unprotected in the open country. The deity speaks to the king and promises him that he will inherit the throne. In Gen 21:17-18 Yahweh speaks similarly to Hagar. The Disputation Question is a means of persuading Hagar in the opening of the oracle, in which she is assured that her son will not die of exposure in the open country, that he will be made into a great nation. Just as the royal ancestor Abram will be made a great nation (Gen 12:2) so the royal ancestor Ishmael will be made a great nation (see Gen 21:13). Just as Yahweh protects and wages peace for Isaac, a descendant of Abraham in the line that becomes the nation of Jacob/Israel, so Yahweh here wages peace and protects Ishmael, another descendant of Abraham in the line that becomes the nation of Ishmaelites.

Before discussing the *Sitz im Text* of this oracle a few more words need to be said about the Disputation Question in Gen 21:17. Understanding Gen 21:17 as a Disputation Question helps resolve what has been seen as a translation problem in Gen 21:16. In Gen 21:15-16 the narrator says that when Hagar ran out of provisions she put the child under one of the bushes and went and sat down a good way off "about the distance of a bowshot." (It is interesting here that a war image is evoked as a measure of distance and that Ishmael when he grew up "became an expert with the bow.") She did not want to see the death of the child. As she sat over against him, "She lifted up her voice and wept" (ותשא את קלה ותבך), vs. 16b. This phrase is often emended to read, "he (i.e., the child) lifted up his voice and wept" (וישא את קלה ויבך)[24] in order to bring it into conformity with vs. 17 which states that "God heard the voice of the lad." It is our contention, however, that the phrase should not be emended. The Disputation Question in the War Oracle is a response to Hagar's weeping in order to persuade her that she need not fear. The narrator is telling us in vss. 16b and 17a that God heard the crying of both the mother Hagar and the infant Ishmael; the weeping of the mother and child are referred to in the War Oracle: Hagar's weeping in the Disputation Question and the child's crying in the Basis of Assurance.

This War Oracle, somewhat distinctive in structure and having affinities with the Esarhaddon oracles, concerns the general protection of the king.[25] We now need to examine the *Sitz im Text* of this oracle. The setting is somewhat complex. On the one hand, it has connections with Gen 15 in that it helps resolve the issue of who will be Abraham's heir, Isaac born to Sarah or Ishmael, the son of the slave woman Hagar. The question of who will be Abraham's legitimate heir is resolved. On the other hand, these events culminating in the War Oracle become a sign to King Abimelech and the commander of his army, Phicol, that Yahweh is with Abraham; this recognition by Abimelech and his entourage also followed the War Oracle offered to Isaac in Gen 26:24. The War Oracle here, like the War Oracles in Gen 15:1b and 26:24, is used rhetorically in the text as evidence of the way Yahweh is waging peace for the royal ancestor Abraham and his descendants.

Gen 21:1-15 concerns the jealousy of Sarah for her son Isaac that he be Abraham's heir. She requests that Abraham expel the slave woman Hagar and Abraham's son born to her, Ishmael, from the household so that a rival to Abraham's succession be removed. Abraham is reluctant to expel his own offspring from his household but does so after Yahweh assures him that Ishmael's offspring will also be made a great nation. The War Oracle addressed to Hagar, like the oracle addressed to Esarhaddon's mother, assures the mother that the royal ancestor will be protected so that he will be made a great nation. In the narrative the War Oracle functions as a means of demonstrating how Yahweh protects and assures the survival of Abraham's offspring; the War Oracle in Gen 26:24 functions similarly as a means of demonstrating how Yahweh protects and assures the survival of Isaac, Abraham's offspring, through whom his descendants will be named (Gen 26:12).

This entire incident is narrated in the middle of an account concerning Abraham and Abimelech (Gen 20:1-18 and 21:22-34), an account that parallels the similar story of Isaac and Abimelech in Gen 26. Just as here a conflict developed between Abraham and Abimelech because Abraham had tried to pass off Sarah as his sister, so a conflict arose between Isaac and Abimelech because Isaac had tried to pass off Rebekah as his sister. Furthermore, Abraham became prosperous in spite of the ruse, just as Isaac became prosperous. Yahweh was caring for them. Interestingly, in Gen 21 as in Gen 26, it is after the War Oracle that Abimelech the king and Phicol the commander of his army come to the patriarch and confess that Yahweh is with him. In both places Abimelech makes a covenant with the patriarch (compare Gen 21:22-34 with Gen 26:26-33). In both chapters the War Oracle seems to have a similar function. The War Oracle functions in both stories as a narrative device to show how Yahweh is intervening in the affairs of Abraham and his descendants to wage peace. Because of this intervention Abraham and his descendants become a witness to a foreign nation and its king of God's activity on behalf of Abraham and his offspring. In neither chapter are we to understand that Abimelech heard the War Oracles and therefore became convinced of Yahweh's presence with either Abraham or Isaac. The War Oracles are appropriate forms for the narrator to use to express how Yahweh is with the ancestors of Jacob/Israel. He is with them as is a deity who fights for and protects a king. In Genesis, however, the War Oracles are not used to promise the defeat of the enemy so much as to promise a future for the offspring of Abraham. This future is envisaged as a time when the nations will find blessing and peace (cf. Gen 12:2).

In summary, the War Oracle addressed to Hagar has a somewhat distinctive structure. It has parallels with the oracles addressed to Esarhaddon discussed in Appendix III, especially the oracle given in response to the concern of the mother of Esarhaddon for her son. Like those oracles it concerns the general protection of the king, in this case Ishmael who will become a great nation. The War Oracle serves two complementary purposes. First, it serves to express the action of Yahweh to protect the offspring of Abraham when friction occurs in Abraham's household over who will be his heir—his son Isaac born to Sarah or his son Ishmael born to the slave woman Hagar. Second, it is an appropriate genre for the narrator to use to express how Yahweh is present in the life of Abraham: he is there like a deity who protects a king. It is for this reason that Abimelech and his army commander can confess that Yahweh is with Abraham. Yahweh assures the survival of Abraham and his offspring as a deity assures the survival of a king. What is envisaged in these stories of Israel's ancestors, however, is not a survival that anticipates the continual defeat of the enemy but a survival that insures blessing and peace among the nations.

Gen 46:3-4

As the book of Genesis draws to a close, a War Oracle is spoken to the father of the nation Israel, Jacob himself.[26] This oracle assures Jacob that he need not fear to journey into the territory of the enemy Egypt for Yahweh will ensure his future by making him a great nation. He will not be involved in warfare as an active warrior but he will die in peace; indeed his son Joseph will close his eyes.

This oracle comes to Jacob after his sons inform him that Joseph is alive, and while he is making preparations to journey to Egypt. The oracle comes to Jacob at Beersheba, the place where Isaac received a War Oracle (Gen 26:23). It comes as Jacob is offering sacrifices at the place where Isaac built an altar after he had received the War Oracle (Gen 26:25). That Yahweh spoke to Jacob in "visions of the night" (במראת הלילה) is consistent with the mode of communicating War Oracles in Genesis and communicating War Oracles to kings. Yahweh addresses Jacob by calling his name, "Jacob, Jacob." As we have noted, this personal address to the recipient of an oracle is characteristic of the War Oracle used to address a king and is particularly characteristic of oracles spoken to the exilic and post-exilic community. After Jacob responds to Yahweh with the words, "Here am I," Yahweh delivers a War Oracle which can be outlined as follows:

(a)   SELF-DESIGNATION OF THE DEITY

I am the God, the God of your father;
אנכי האל אלהי אביך

(b)   ASSURANCE

do not be afraid
אל תירא

(c)   OBJECT OF FEAR

to go down to Egypt;
מרדה מצרימה

(d)   PROMISE

for I will make of you a great nation. I will go down with you to Egypt, and I will also bring you up again; and Joseph's hand shall close your eyes.
כי לגוי גדול אשימך שם אנכי ארד עמך מצרימה ואנכי אעלך גם עלה ויוסף
ישית ידו על עיניך

This oracle like the one Isaac received at Beersheba has a Self-Designation of the Deity.[27] The Assurance is the typical אל תירא. There is no Basis of Assurance but the Promise introduced by כי also functions as a Basis of Assurance (cf. Isa 44:1-5). Here the Promise includes the common motif of the Basis of Assurance that Yahweh will be "with" (עם) the recipient of the oracle. The Object of Fear is not typical of the other oracles in Genesis but sometimes occurs in royal War Oracles (see Isa 7:4-9 and 37:6-7). The use of this element anticipates the next major episode in the story, Israel's enslavement in Egypt where the Egyptian forces become a threatening enemy of Israel. According to the Promise formulated in the first person, Yahweh will make Jacob a great nation. This element reiterates the promise to Abraham (Gen 12:2) of offspring, anticipates the war that Yahweh will fight for Israel in Egypt, and says that Jacob will die in peace, with his son Joseph closing his eyes. Jacob will not die the violent death of a warrior; like the other ancestors in Genesis, he will die in peace, for Yahweh is waging peace for the fathers of Israel.

Little more needs to be said about this oracle other than that it functions as an appropriate form in its *Sitz im Text,* in the narrative to promise Jacob the protection of the deity as Jacob prepares to journey into the land that will become his enemy. Yahweh will protect this ancestor, as he would protect a king in the land of the nation that will be his enemy. After receiving the oracle Jacob sets out for his destination with "all his offspring" (וכל זרעו אתו), 46:6. While Abraham and Isaac were promised an abundant posterity, Jacob now has an abundant offspring which will become even more numerous in Egypt (Exod 1:12). Those who know the story are aware that the "offspring" are journeying ultimately into exile and oppression. However, they are a royal community for whom Yahweh will fight. In the next chapter we will look at a War Oracle in Exodus which precedes Yahweh's victory over Pharoah's army and Israel's exodus from Egypt.

Conclusion

In this chapter we have argued that War Oracles in the Genesis stories of Israel's origins are similar in function to War Oracles in Second Isaiah and other proto-apocalyptic texts. Just as War Oracles are used in Second Isaiah after Israel's warfare is over, so War Oracles appear in Genesis after Abraham's warfare has ceased. Just as the exilic and post-exilic communities are addressed as royalty who themselves will not be active warriors in battle, so in the book of Genesis the ancestors of Israel are addressed as royalty for whom Yahweh will fight. Yahweh is a god who wages peace for the ancestors.[28] He protects in adversity and conflict so that his people, who need not struggle, become a "blessing" to the nations around them. The story of Abimelech's recognition of the presence of Yahweh with these royal ancestors of Jacob/Israel is like Second Isaiah's vision of Jacob/Israel becoming a witness to the nations. While the War

Oracles in the proto-apocalyptic literature promise the restoration of the offspring, these war oracles promise an abundant offspring to the ancestors. In short these War Oracles addressed to the ancestors in the stories of Israel's origins are functionally similar to War Oracles in proto-apocalyptic texts. While royal War Oracles could be used in the community's vision of itself as it looked to the future, royal War Oracles could also be used by the community in its vision of the past.

As the book of Genesis closes, the promise of a great posterity is reaching fulfillment. However, the abundant offspring of Abraham will find themselves enslaved by the enemy in Egypt away from the Promised Land, just as the exilic community finds itself scattered in lands of oppression.

CHAPTER VIII

THE WAR ORACLE AND THE ROYAL COMMUNITY IN THE BOOK OF EXODUS

Introduction

The book of Exodus contains one War Oracle (Exod 14:13-14) which Moses delivers to
the people before Yahweh's victory for them at the Sea. This oracle should also be
understood as a royal oracle because it orders the people, like kings, not to fight.[1] The
Sitz im Text of the oracle also associates it with royalty because the vocation of the
community is to praise Yahweh for the victory he achieves on behalf of the people.[2]

Exod 14:13-14: The Structure

The structure of the War Oracle in Exodus 14:13-14 can be outlined as follows:

(a)   ASSURANCE

      Fear not,
      אל תיראו

(b)   DIRECTIVE

      stand firm,
      התיצבו

(c)   BASIS OF ASSURANCE

      and see the salvation of the LORD, which he will work for you today; for the
      Egyptians whom you see today, you shall never see again.
      וראו את ישועת יהוה אשר יעשה לכם היום כי אשר ראיתם את מצרים היום לא
      תסיפו לראתם עוד עד עולם

(d)   ORDERS

      The LORD will be fight for you and you have only to be still.
      יהוה ילחם לכם ואתם תחרישון

The structure contains many of the elements that we have associated with offensive war
situations in the Deuteronomic History, i.e., it lacks an Object of Fear; it has a
Directive; and it introduces the Basis of Assurance with the imperative of ראה[3] (cf. Josh
8:1-2). While this is not an offensive war situation, we noted that War Oracles addressed
to kings who are in a defensive situation sometimes are constructed with elements
typical of the language of war in offensive situations. The deity is on the offensive for

143

the king (cf. Isa 7:4-9).[4] The Orders which command the people not to fight are typical
of the genre when a king is addressed (cf. 2 Chr 20:15-17). The word used in the
Directive "stand firm" (התיצבו) is typical of military vocabulary.[5] For example, in Jer
46:3-4 Jeremiah uses the word in a Directive given to the army,

> Prepare buckler and shield,
>> and advance for battle!
>
> Harness the horses;
>> mount, O horsemen!
>
> Take your stations (התיצבו) with
>> your helmets,
>
>> polish your spears,
>
>> put on your coats of mail![6]

Israel, directed in this oracle to "take its station," is not to do so as an active warrior but
in the passive stance of a king who does not fight. In this military situation, then, Israel
is addressed as royalty.

Exod 14:13-14: The Setting

The *Sitz im Text* of this oracle is straightforward. Israel is threatened by an attack
from Pharoah and his army (Exod 14:13-14). In response to this military threat Moses
delivers a War Oracle to the people directing them to take their stand and ordering them
to be still. Like kings they are not to fight; Yahweh will fight for them. Immediately
after the oracle is an account of how Yahweh gave victory to the Israelites by defeating
the Egyptians (Exod 14:15-31).

Israel does not participate in the fighting with Yahweh; Yahweh achieves the victory
himself on behalf of his people. Interestingly, after the victory, Moses and the people
sing a hymn of praise to Yahweh (Exod 15:1-18). This is the vocation of a king, i.e., to
offer praise to the deity who gives him victory (see above Chaps. III & IV). The royal
community Jacob/Israel had such a vocation in Second Isaiah; the people were to herald
the victory of Yahweh.

Conclusion

In Exodus Abraham's offspring are addressed with War Oracles just as Jacob/Israel
the offspring of Abraham, Yahweh's friend, was addressed with War Oracles in Second

Isaiah. This Exodus oracle which orders Israel not to fight and which culminates in Israel praising the victory of Yahweh is like those War Oracles in Second Isaiah (Isa 41:8-16) which order Israel not to fight but to celebrate Yahweh's coming victory as heralds of good tidings. Again we notice that royal War Oracles are used both in the prophetic vision of the future victory of Yahweh on behalf of his people and in the celebration of the victory of Yahweh on behalf of the community in the period of its origins.

CONCLUSION

This form critical study has focused on the use of conventional language in the Hebrew Scriptures associated with the formula "fear not." It has been argued that the phrase occurs with other regularly recurring elements so that it is possible to speak of a stereotypical structure of language used to comfort a warrior or warriors before a battle. The recognition of the function of the "fear not" language has not been dependent on identifying an institutional setting (a *Sitz im Leben*); rather, it has relied on the rhetorical settings (the *Sitze im Text*) in which the "fear not" pericopes occur. The study, then, has not been a search for the origins of the form but an examination of its life in the literary traditions of Israel. By concentrating on the application of the form rather than the reconstruction of the institutional life of Israel, the study has unfolded the richness of the language. Too often form critical studies have distorted their significance of forms by treating them in isolation from their surrounding contexts and binding them in the strait jacket of a reconstructed *Sitz im Leben*.

We argued that the structure of the language associated with "fear not" will be affected by the specific occasion of its use. There are particular ways of structuring the language for defensive battles, offensive battles, the appointment of a warrior to his vocation and the subject of warfare generally. We also maintained that this language in the Hebrew Scriptures cannot be understood only as a divine form of speech. In the Deuteronomic History a human being can use this "fear not" language as an appropriate form of address to comfort a warrior. To be sure in the Hebrew Scriptures these words of comfort to a warrior are most often spoken by Yahweh or his representative (e.g., a prophet) but the form is not used exclusively in this way.

The stereotypical language associated with "fear not," then, can be used by the deity or by human beings to comfort and give orders to conventional warriors before active engagement in battle. We also noted, however, that the language can be used to comfort less conventional warriors. Elijah is comforted as a prophetic warrior who fights for Yahweh not with conventional weapons but as an intermediary of Yahweh pronouncing his words of judgment that prophesy destruction of the enemy. It is precisely in this sense that "fear not" language is used in the book of Jeremiah, especially in the call of Jeremiah where he is commissioned as a prophetic warrior of Yahweh to align himself against the nations and against Judah.

We also noted that the conventional war language using the formula "fear not" was employed by Isaiah to comfort the kings Ahaz and Hezekiah. These kings were not conventional warriors. They were not given orders to fight; the deity promised that he alone would fight for the king. This use of the form by Isaiah is similar to War Oracles in extra-biblical texts dated roughly during the same period as Isaiah. Indeed, War Oracles addressed to kings are distinctive. Royal warriors are not ordered to fight as conventional warriors do but are promised that the deity will fight alone to give the king victory. If given orders at all, kings are ordered to remain uninvolved. That the king's role is to offer praise to the deity is evident from the use of the form in the Chronicler's History and in Haggai where the form is used in connection with the building of the temple as a citadel of defense against the enemy.

We noted in the Chronicler's History that the use of the royal War Oracle was extended to the community. This use of the form became particularly prominent in Second Isaiah and in other proto-apocalyptic texts where the community is addressed as king, i.e., the community is not given orders to fight but is promised that the deity alone will act to ensure victory for the royal community. Interestingly, this royal community is associated with the patriarchs, most notably Abraham. Also, what is promised to the royal community is the restoration of offspring—a motif characteristic of the patriarchal promise.

The association of the community in proto-apocalyptic texts with Abraham and the promise of offspring to the community for whom Yahweh would fight to insure victory has interesting parallels in the patriarchal narratives themselves where the royal War Oracle is employed. Here the patriarchs are comforted by Yahweh who wages peace for them so that they will become a blessing among the nations. It is in these royal War Oracles in the patriarchal narratives that Yahweh also promises the ancestors of Israel that they will have an abundant offspring. The form has thus been used similarly in the narratives about the origins of Israel and in passages in proto-apocalyptic texts referring to the future envisioned for the offspring of Abraham.

It should not be surprising that the War Oracle is also used in the book of Exodus in connection with the victory par excellence which Yahweh fought on behalf of Israel when he defeated the Egyptians at the Sea. There the community, like a king, is not ordered into battle because, "the LORD will fight for you, and you have only to be still" (Exod 14:14).

Our study, then, has dealt with conventional and stereotypical "fear not" language as it has been manifested in the literary traditions in the Hebrew Scriptures. Our stress on the typical has not led us to the static but to the creative uses of conventional language. Our understanding of the typical has given us insights into the new and the unique.

Having completed a study such as this will produce other questions for the reader and the author alike. There are two basic sets of questions that can and must be raised. These two sets of questions are not mutually exclusive but they are different, and the answers to one set of questions will not necessarily give us insight into the other. Both sets of questions concern the quest for origins, but the avenues for understanding those origins are significantly different.

(1)   There are those who are primarily concerned with the questions concerning the history of ancient Israel—with "what really happened." These sorts of questions lead one away from the text to pose questions about the cultural and political life of the community presupposed by the text. In our study we have avoided such questions although form criticism as it is traditionally practiced seeks to understand the institutional life of Israel. Our study could be a starting point for those interested in these issues, for example, as it relates to kingship. We have argued that "fear not" language is used both in Israel and the surrounding nations to comfort a king and to promise him victory. One could pose questions about the occasion of such an oracle. Could it possibly have been used in connection with the New Year's Festival, as one author at least has suggested?[1] One might use the results of this study to provide data for a study of ancient Israel in an attempt to explain the origins of the text by coming to a clearer understanding of the nation of Israel presupposed by it and in particular the role of the king and his relation to the cult.

(2)   On the other hand there are those who are interested not so much in the world behind the text as in the world created by the text, i.e., the world that has its origins in Israel's imagination. The results of our study can also provide insight into that world— what one might call the mythic consciousness of ancient Israel.

Clearly in Israel's imagining about her past and about her future, warfare was a central motif which undoubtedly can be accounted for by her experience of warfare in her struggle to survive amid much stronger military powers in the ancient world. Our study suggests that in Israel's wondering about her past and future, two paradigmatic warriors emerge. There is paradigmatic Joshua who is actively involved in fighting battles which eventuate in Israel's winning the land. Interestingly, Israel employs this paradigm in its remembrance of Jeremiah, a warrior prophet whose words of judgment precede the destruction of the state at the hands of the enemy and loss of the land. On the other hand there is paradigmatic Abraham. Abraham is not a conventional warrior. It is Yahweh who wages peace for him among the nations and who promises him a great posterity. Israel also remembers in the stories of her origins that Yahweh as a warrior delivered his people at the sea; like royalty the people had only to be still and watch the victory of Yahweh over the Egyptians. In the exilic and post-exilic periods in Israel's imagining about the future, the paradigm of the non-conventional warrior Abraham stands at the center of Israel's attention as she wonders about the future victory of Yahweh that will result in the restoration of offspring and a return to the land.

The results of this study, then, can be used to move in two directions: to provide evidence of ancient social institutions or to provide insight into Israel's imaginings about survival.

APPENDIX I

THE CALL OF EZEKIEL

Within the long call narrative of the prophet Ezekiel there are two verses (2:6-7) which contain the phrase "fear not." These verses are structurally similar to the elements of address to a warrior that we have been considering and can be outlined as follows:

(a) ADDRESS

>   And you, son of man,
>   ואתה בן אדם

(b) ASSURANCE

>   be not afraid
>   אל תירא

(c) OBJECT OF FEAR

>   of them,
>   מהם

(d) OBJECT OF FEAR

>   and of their words
>   ומדבריהם

(e) ASSURANCE

>   be not afraid,
>   אל תירא

(f) BASIS OF ASSURANCE

>   though briers and thorns are with you and you sit upon scorpions;
>   כי סרבים וסלונים אותך ואל עקרבים אתה יושב

(g) OBJECT OF FEAR

>   of their words
>   מדבריהם

(h) ASSURANCE

>   be not afraid,
>   אל תירא

150

(i)   OBJECT OF FEAR

and at their looks
ומפניהם

(j)   ASSURANCE

be not dismayed,
אל תחת

(k)   BASIS OF ASSURANCE

for they are a rebellious house.
כי בית מרי המה

(l)   ORDERS

And you shall speak my words to them, whether they hear or refuse to
hear; for they are a rebellious house.
ודברת את דברי אליהם אם ישמעו ואם יחדלו כי מרי המה

There are some parallels between these verses and the language of address to a
warrior, but there are also some peculiarities. The Orders for Ezekiel to speak Yahweh's
words are similar to the Orders given to Jeremiah (Jer 1:7, 9). The four Assurances and
the four Objects of Fear are not common in the texts we have considered (but compare
Jer 42:10-11).[1] Furthermore, the two Bases of Assurance are strange when they are
compared with this element as we have outlined it in the body of this study. While both
are introduced by כי, neither gives a reason for Ezekiel not to be afraid. The first so-
called Basis of Assurance simply states that Ezekiel is not to be afraid although briers
and thorns are with him and he sits on scorpions. The second Basis of Assurance simply
identifies Israel as a rebellious house. (This same phrase is repeated at the end of the
Orders in vs. 8). The opening direct address to Ezekiel is not typical of the genre
although the pericope in Jer 1:17-19 opens with ואתה (cf. Isa 41:8). In short, while these
verses appear to be related to other "fear not" pericopes we have considered, they are
structurally somewhat distinct.

The distinctiveness of these verses, however, goes beyond structure. There is
nothing in the content of the verses nor in their larger literary context which would
suggest a background of war.

How, then, are we to account for this "fear not" formula in the call of Ezekiel and
for the other structural elements that are typical of the language of address to a

warrior? One might argue that "fear not" occurs here because the phrase can be used
generally to offer words of comfort, as we have indicated in Chapter I. That
explanation, however, fails to take into consideration the other elements used here which
are typical of the language associated with war that we have been considering. There is
another explanation that can account for the similarities as well as the differences in the
application of the stereotypical language used to address a warrior in the call of
Ezekiel. W. Zimmerli in his commentary on Ezekiel has argued that Ezekiel has been
influenced by the literary prophets that preceded him.[2] This is particularly true of the
"very marked connection between Ezekiel and Jeremiah," and is especially true of the
close connection of the call of Jeremiah with Ezek 2-3.[3] He suggests that it is possible
that Ezekiel knows at least some of the Jeremianic tradition not in oral but in written
form.[4] We would argue that the close connection between Ezek 2:6-7 and the address to
Jeremiah as a prophetic warrior (Jer 1:7-8 and 17-19)[5] can also be explained by the
dependence of Ezekiel (or the redactor of Ezekiel)[6] on the written transmission of
Jeremiah's words. In constructing Ezekiel's call narrative, the "fear not" (אל תירא, Jer
1:7-8) and the "be not dismayed" (אל תחת, Jer 1:17-19) language from the call narrative
of Jeremiah has been appropriated. The peculiarities in the structure of the other
elements used with these two phrases as well as the lack of awareness of the war
connotations of this language are to be explained by the fact that the person responsible
for the final editing of the book of Ezekiel was not aware of the military setting from
which this language emerged. The fact that the book of Ezekiel shows such little
dependence on or knowledge of the Deuteronomic tradition[7] to which Jeremiah was so
closely related may also help explain how the language from a written text of Jeremiah
could be appropriated without its military connotations. Such an explanation helps
explain the close links of Ezek 2:6-7 with the language of address to a warrior as well as
the divergences from it.

APPENDIX II

"FEAR NOT" ORACLES ADDRESSED TO ESARHADDON AND ASHURBANIPAL

Introduction

In Chapter III we discussed "fear not" oracles addressed to King Zakir and to King Ashurbanipal. We maintained that these three extra-biblical texts followed the same conventions in structure and function as the oracles which Isaiah spoke to King Hezekiah (2 Kgs 19:6//Isa 37:6) and King Ahaz (Isa 7:4-9). The structure contained either Orders that the king not fight or a Promise that the deity would fight for the king; and the function was to assure the king in the face of military threat to his kingship. In this Appendix we will consider other extra-biblical "fear not" oracles addressed to Esarhaddon.[1] These texts are not integral to our study but throw light on some of the peculiar features of the genre as it is employed in Second Isaiah and Genesis.[2] The discussion here is in no way intended to be definitive.

Oracles Concerning Esarhaddon

Five oracles addressed to Esarhaddon were alluded to in the body of the book. While these oracles seem to have affinities with "fear not" texts in the Hebrew Scriptures, especially in Second Isaiah and Genesis, they present peculiar problems. The structure of the oracles is rather fluid; they do not fit as neatly into the pattern of the language of address to the king as warrior that we encountered in the Hebrew Scriptures or in other extra-biblical texts (see Chapter III). Furthermore, the context in which the oracles were given is not stated; they are part of a collection. In no instance does it appear that any of the oracles was addressed to the king in response to a specific military threat to kingship as was the case in "fear not" texts associated with Ahaz, Hezekiah, Zakir and Ashurbanipal. All the oracles seem to be concerned with a threat to kingship in general and offer the deity's protection of the king by stating that the deity will fight for him.

The oracles are outlined below and for convenience of discussion are labeled by numbers.[3]

CHART A

ORACLE #1

From the woman Ishtar-la-tashiat of Arbela
Col. i, 1.5 to 1.30

(a) ADDRESS

[Esarhad]don, king of the lands,

(b) ASSURANCE

fear not !

(c) BASIS OF ASSURANCE

That wind which blows against you—I need only say a word and I can bring it to an end. Your enemies, like a (young) boar in the month of Simanu, will flee even at your approach.

(d) SELF-DESIGNATION OF THE DEITY

I am the great Belet—I am the goddess Ishtar of Arbela, she who has destroyed your enemies at your approach.

(e) DISPUTATION QUESTION

What order have I given you which you did not rely upon?

(f) SELF-DESIGNATION OF THE DEITY

I am Ishtar of Arbela !

(g) PROMISE

I shall lie in wait for your enemies, I shall give them to you. I, Ishtar of Arbela, will go before you and behind you.

(h) ASSURANCE

Fear not !

(i) ADDRESS

You who are paralyzed (saying), "Only in crying Woe can I either get up or sit down."

ORACLE #2

Name of person who delivered oracle missing
Col. i, 1.34 . . . (end of text is fragmentary)

(a) ADDRESS

O king of Assyria,

(b)   ASSURANCE

      fear not!

(c)   PROMISE

      The enemy of the king of Assyria I will deliver to slaughter.

ORACLE #3

From the woman Baia of Arbela
Col. ii, 1.16 to 1.40

(a)   ASSURANCE

      Fear not,

(b)   ADDRESS

      Esarhaddon!

(c)   SELF-DESIGNATION OF THE DEITY

      I, the god Bel, am speaking to you.

(d)   BASIS OF ASSURANCE

      I watch over your inner heart as would your mother who brought you forth. Sixty great gods are standing together with me and protect you. The god Sin is at your right, the god Shamash at your left. The sixty great gods are standing around you, ranged for battle.

(e)   DIRECTIVE

      Do not trust human beings! Lift up your eyes to me, trust me!

(f)   SELF-DESIGNATION OF THE DEITY

      I am Ishtar of Arbela;

(g)   BASIS OF ASSURANCE

      I have turned Ashur's favor to you. When you were small I *chose* you.

(h)   ASSURANCE

      Fear not!

(i)   DIRECTIVE

      Praise me!

(j)   DISPUTATION QUESTION

      Where is there any enemy who *overcame* you while I remained quiet?

(k)   PROMISE

      Those who are (now) behind will (soon) be the leaders.

(l)   SELF-DESIGNATION OF THE DEITY

I am the god Nabu, god of the stylus.

(m)   DIRECTIVE

Praise me!

ORACLE #4

Name of person who delivered the oracle is missing
Col. iii, 1.15 . . . (end of oracle obscure).

(a)   SELF-DESIGNATION OF THE DEITY

I am Ishtar of Arbela,

(b)   ADDRESS

O Esarhaddon, king of Assyria.

(c)   BASIS OF ASSURANCE

In the cities Ashur, Nineveh, Calah, Arbela shall grant you many days.

(d)   SELF-DESIGNATION OF THE DEITY

I am the great midwife (who helped at your birth), the one who gave you suck, who has established your rule under the *wide* heavens for many days, endless years;

(e)   BASIS OF ASSURANCE

from a golden chamber in the heavens I will watch. I will light a lamp of *elmeshu*-stone for Esarhaddon, king of Assyria. I will watch him like my very own crown.

(f)   ASSURANCE

Fear not,

(g)   ADDRESS

O king!

(h)   BASIS OF ASSURANCE

Because I have spoken to you (in an oracle), I will not abandon you. Because I have encouraged you, I shall not let you come to shame. I will help you cross the river safely.

(i)   ADDRESS

O Esarhaddon, legitimate heir, son of the goddess Ninlil!

(j)   BASIS OF ASSURANCE

I am . . . for you.

(k)   PROMISE

> With my own hands, your foes I shall annihilate (lines 11 and 12 obscure). O Esarhaddon, in the city of Ashur I shall grant you long days, endless years.

(l)   ADDRESS

> O Esarhaddon

(m)   BASIS OF ASSURANCE

> in Arbela, I am your good shield.

(n)   ADDRESS

> O Esarhaddon, legitimate heir, son of the goddess Ninlil,

(o)   BASIS OF ASSURANCE

> I am thinking of [you]. I love [you] very much.

ORACLE #5

From the woman Belit-abisha of Arbela
Col. v, 1.12 to 1.25

(a)   SELF-DESIGNATION OF THE DEITY

> I, the Lady of Arbela, (say) to the king's mother:

(b)   DISPUTATION

> "Because you have complained against me saying 'He who is at the right and he who is at the left you hold on your lap, but where is my offspring? You make him run about (unprotected) in the open country!'"

(c)   ADDRESS

> Now, O king,

(d)   ASSURANCE

> Fear not!

(e)   BASIS OF ASSURANCE

> Yours is the kingship! Yours is the might!

That these oracles are concerned with the threat to kingship occasioned by war is evident from allusions in the texts themselves.[4] In Oracle #1 the goddess says, "Your enemies, like a (young) boar in the month of Semanu, will flee even at your approach," and "I shall lie in wait for your enemies, I shall give them to you." In Oracle #2 she says, "The enemy of the king of Assyria I will deliver to slaughter." The Basis of Assurance in Oracle #3 states, "The sixty great gods are standing around you, ranged for battle," and the Disputation Question asks the king, "Where is there any enemy who *overcame* you while I remained quiet?" In the Promise announced in Oracle #5 the goddess says, "With my own hands, your foes I shall annihilate."

Again it should be emphasized that none of these oracles was addressed to Esarhaddon in response to a specific military threat, but all offer protection to Esarhaddon's kingship no matter what military threat to kingship might arise. This assurance of protection to Esarhaddon's kingship is particularly evident in Oracle #5 given in response to the complaint of the Queen mother. Here the goddess says to Esarhaddon, "Yours is the kingship! Yours is the might!"

The structure of these texts, more fluid than that of the texts considered in the body of the study, evinces some of the elements of the language of address to a warrior; some elements are lacking and others are added. These anomalies can be explained in part by the situation. None of the oracles is occasioned by a specific military threat to kingship; all concern the general protection of the king.

The missing Object of Fear, the use of a Promise rather than Orders, and the use of the Address are all features that we have associated with the genre in royal contexts.[5]

What makes these texts most distinctive, however, is the presence of the elements which we have called the Self-Designation of the Deity and the Disputation Question.[6] Both of these elements add strength to the Basis of Assurance. By identifying herself the deity reinforces the assuring words "fear not" as, e.g., in Oracle #1 where she says, "I am the great Belet—I am the goddess Ishtar of Arbela, she who has destroyed your enemies at your approach." The Disputation Question has a similar function of adding support to the words "fear not," as in Oracle #3 where the question is raised, "Where is there any enemy who *overcame* you while I remained quiet?" Indeed it appears that the major purpose of all the oracles is to give a basis for the Assurance, "fear not." It is difficult to distinguish between the Basis of Assurance and the Promise. Neither of these two elements has a rigid formulation.

A motif that occurs in these oracles is that the goddess cares for the king as a mother cares for a child and further that the goddess has cared for the king since birth. In Oracle #3 the goddess says, "I watch over your inner heart as would your mother who brought you forth," and in Oracle #4 she says, "I am the great midwife (who helped at your birth), the one who gave you suck . . ." In Oracle #5 the goddess responds to the maternal concern of the queen mother. This emphasis on the maternal concern of the deity is paralleled in Second Isaiah where Yahweh shows a similar concern for the community since its "birth" from the loins of Abraham.

Oracle #3 contains what we have called a Directive; but this element, which occurs three times, is not a Directive for battle. It directs the king to praise the deity and not to trust human beings. Here again the emphasis seems to be to assure the king by directing him to put his full trust in the deity. We noted above that when the genre was used to address kings, the king was not to place his trust in human participation in battle (see Chp. III) but was to lead the community in praising the deity (see Chp. IV).

In summary, then, these oracles, while related to the language of address to the king as warrior, are distinctive. They do not concern a specific military threat, and their structure is more fluid, with some elements missing and others added. It is possible that the oracles addressed to Esarhaddon were once spoken in a cultic ceremony having to do with the renewal of kingship.[7] The details of the specific cultic occasion, however, cannot be reconstructed. Generally, however, it can be said that "fear not" is used in these texts along with other stereotypical formulations to assure the king in the face of a military threat to his kingship.

ENDNOTES

INTRODUCTION

[1]See, e.g., Gerhard von Rad, *Der Heilige Krieg im alten Israel* (Zürich: Zwingli, 1951; also Göttingen: Vandehoeck und Ruprecht, 1969). A translation of this monograph by Edgar W. Conrad and Michael Lattke will be published by JSOT Press.

[2]See, e.g., Patrick D. Miller, *The Divine Warrior in Early Israel* (Cambridge: Harvard University, 1973); and Frank Moore Cross, *Canaanite Myth and Hebrew Epic* (Cambridge: Harvard University, 1973) 91-111.

[3]"Fear not" is not a formula in the Old Testament used exclusively in contexts of war. Our study will focus on the formula as part of a larger structure in conventional language associated with war. The formula is sometimes used in theophanic contexts to quell the fear raised by the appearance of the deity. This use of the formula plays a relatively minor role in the Hebrew Scriptures as Joachim Becker observes: "Die einzigen Stellen des AT, an denen 'al-tîrā' den wegen der offenbarung des Gottlichen erschreckenden Menschen beruhigen soll sind Ri 6,23; Ex 20,20 und Dn 10, 12.19." (*Gottesfurcht im Alten Testament* [AnBib 25; Rom: Päpstliches Bibelinstitut, 1965] 53.) The phrase also occurs in texts associated with the birth of a child (Gen 35:17 and 1 Sam 4:20) and functions as general words of assurance in other contexts (e.g., Pss 49:17; 91:5; Prov 3:25; Job 5:21,22; 11:15; 1 Sam 28:13; 1 Kgs 17:3; Ruth 3:11; etc.).

[4]"Das priesterliche Heilsorakel," ZAW 52 (1934) 81-92 (reprinted in *Gesammelte Studien zum Alten Testament* [TBü 21; München: Chr. Kaiser, 1964] 217-31). In his *Studien zu Deuterojesaja* ([BWANT 77; Stuttgart: Kohlhammer, 1938] 6-18; reprinted in [TBü 20; Munchen: Chr. Kaiser, 1963] 14-26) he broadens his understanding of the structure of the so-called *Heilsorakel* and the phrase "fear not" ceases to be as crucial an element as in his earlier articles.

[5]Claus Westermann's work has been the most influential in refining and developing Begrich's thesis concerning Second Isaiah's use of the so-called oracle of salvation. See especially his "Das Heilswort bei Deuterojesajas," EvT 24 (1964) 355-73; "Sprache und Struktur der Prophetie Deuterojesajas," *Forshung am Alten Testament* (TBü 24; München: Chr. Kaiser, 1964) 117-124; and *Isaiah 40-66* (Old Testament Library; Philadelphia: Westminster, 1969) 11-14. For a review of scholarship on the oracle of salvation as well as Schoors' own contribution see Antoon Schoors, *I am God Your Saviour* (VTSup 24; Leiden: Brill, 1973) 1-84.

[6]See my "Second Isaiah and the Priestly Oracle of Salvation," ZAW 93 (1981) 234-46; and "The 'Fear Not' Oracles in Second Isaiah," VT 34 (1984) 129-52.

[7]von Rad, *Der Heilige Krieg*, 9-10.

[8]See, e.g., George W. Anderson, "'AM; KĀHĀL; 'ĒDÂH," *Translating and Understanding the Old Testament: Essays in Honor of Herbert Gordon May* (ed. H. T. Frank and W. L. Reed; New York: Abingdon, 1970) 135-151; and A. D. H. Mayes, "The Period of the Judges and the Rise of the Monarchy," *Israelite and Judean History* (ed. J. H. Hayes and J. M. Miller; Old Testament Library; Philadelphia: Westminster, 1977) 299-308. See also Fritz Stolz *(Jahwes und Israels Kriege* [ATANT 60; Zürich: Theologischer Verlag, 1972]) who argues that there was no unified tradition of holy war because there was no unified confederation of Israel before the institution of kingship.

[9]JBL 87 (1969) 1-19.

CHAPTER I: "FEAR NOT" IN THE DEUTERONOMIC HISTORY

[1]I have followed the MT which reads בידך; RSV translates "into your hands (בידיך) apparently on the basis of the Septuagint, Vulgate and Syriac and the Kethib of the editio Bombergiana Iacobi ben Chajjim, Venetiis 1524/5.

[2]G. von Rad *(Der Heilige Krieg im alten Israel* [Göttingen: Vandenhoeck & Ruprecht, 1969] 7-8) sees this phrase as an important element in the war cry associated with Holy War as it was conducted in the amphictyony.

[3]This is one place in the Hebrew Scriptures where a priest speaks a "fear not" oracle. The setting is not the lament liturgy as one might expect if "fear not" is a key element in the so-called Priestly Oracle of Salvation; the setting concerns the preparation for war.

[4]In Deut 1:20-21 Moses is addressing the community, but in connection with that passage we argued that Moses was relaying the orders he received as a war leader to the community.

[5]RSV translates "then kill him."

[6]The orders occur only in Jer 40:9-10.

[7]Some form critics have argued that the phrase, חזק ואמץ , is a key formula in an "Installation Genre" *(Amtseinsetzung).* See, for example, N. Lohfink, "Die deuteronomistische Darstellung des Übergangs der Führung Israels von Moses auf Josue," *Scholastic* 37 (1962) 32-34. Lohfink (p. 38) identified the *Amtseinsetzung* in Deut 31:23 which he analyzed as consisting of three parts: I. Ermutigsformel (חזק ואמץ), II. Nennung einer Aufgabe (eingeleitet durch: כי אתה), III. Beistandsformel (entscheidendes Element: יהוה עמך). Lohfink's thesis is that this structure provides the literary and theological framework for the Deuteronomists by means of which they linked Joshua and Deuteronomy. D. J. McCarthy's article ("An Installation Genre?" JBL 90 [1971] 31-41) sought to develop Lohfink's thesis. For a criticism of Lohfink's thesis see M. Weinfeld, *Deuteronomy and the Deuteronomic School* (Oxford: Clarendon, 1972) 45ff. It is our contention that in the Deuteronomic History as well as in the larger context of the Hebrew Scriptures the phrase is often linked with חזק ואמץ in conventional language of war and serves as encouragement for a leader(s) who has been given a new task to perform as warrior.

[8]See A. F. Hesse, "חזק, chāzaq" TDOT 4 (1967) 306-7 who says that the imperative of חזק is used as "a formula of encouragement." He adds, "As the *Sitz im Leben* for this imperative, which is frequently combined with the imperative of אמץ, 'amats, we may postulate the rituals of the Yahweh war."

[9]This thesis will be developed more fully in Chp. III.

CHAPTER II: "FEAR NOT" AND THE PROPHETIC WARRIOR

[1]The "fear not" pericopes in Jer 30:10-11 closely paralleled in Jer 46:27-28 will be considered in Chp. VI.

[2]See E. Kutsch, "Gideons Berufung und Alterbau," TLZ 81 (1956) 75-84; and N. Habel, "The Form and Significance of the Call Narratives," ZAW 77 (1965) 297-323. Kutsch argues that the structure of the call *Gattung,* which he finds in Judg 6:11b-17; Exod 3:10-12; 1 Sam 10:1-7 (plus 9:21); and Jer 1:4-10; contains four elements: commission, objection, reassurance and sign. Habel finds the call *Gattung* in Judg 6:11b-17; Exod 3:1-12; Jer 1:4-10; Isa 6:1-13; Ezek 1:1-3:15 and Isa 40:1-11 and identifies six characteristic elements: divine confrontation, introductory word, commission, objection, reassurance and sign.

[3]See H. G. Reventlow, *Liturgie und prophetisches Ich bei Jeremia* (Gerd Mohn: Gütersloher Verlaghaus, 1963) 24ff. For his reconstruction of the call ritual see pp. 70ff.

[4]J. M. Berridge, *Prophet, People, and the Word of Yahweh* (Basel Studies of Theology 4; Zürich: EVZ Verlag, 1970) 26ff.

[5]See, for example, J. R. Lundbom, *Jeremiah: A Study in Ancient Hebrew Rhetoric* (SBLDS 18; Missoula: Scholars, 1975) 96-99.

[6]See for example W. L. Holladay, "The Background of Jeremiah's Self-Understanding: Moses, Samuel and Psalm 22," JBL 83 (1964) 159-61.

[7]I have gained important insights about the structure of Jer 1 from Lundbom (see note 5). However, my form critical observations have led me to a slightly different understanding of the rhetorical structure of the chapter.

[8]The formula in 1:13 contains the word שנית. The significance of this word is discussed below.

[9]Both Kutsch and Habel have seen this objection as an important element in the call *Gattung*.

[10]See J. Bright, *Jeremiah* (AB 21; Garden City: Doubleday, 1965) 7-8.

[11]The chiasmic structure is similar to that of Lundbom (*Jeremiah*, 98) who understands it as follows:
  A Articulation of the Call (4-10)
  B   Vision of the Call (11-12)
  B[1] Vision of the Promise (13-14)
  A[1] Articulation of the Promise (15-16)

[12]This pericope which is sometimes understood as the so-called Oracle of Salvation has been interpreted as relating to war. See Berridge, *Prophet, People*, 199 and Reventlow, *Liturgie*, 61.

[13]Some have noted the military connotations of the phrase, תאזר מתניך , "gird up your loins." See Berridge (*Prophet, People*, 199) who cites 1 Kgs 20:11 and Isa 5:27 as passages where the notion of girding up one's loins is used in contexts associated with the preparation for war.

[14]See above note 2.

[15](London: SCM, 1981).

[16]Ibid., 33.

[17]The call of Ezekiel which also occurs at the beginning of the book has some parallels with the call of Jeremiah including the use of the formula, "fear not." It is our contention, however, that the war connotations of Ezekiel's call arise from an attempt to imitate the call of Jeremiah and not from a clear understanding of the formula "fear not" as a formula associated with war. See Appendix I.

[18]RSV translates "set over."

CHAPTER III: WAR ORACLES ADDRESSED TO KINGS

[1]See the discussion of this pericope in Chp. I.

[2]We argued above that in the Deuteronomic History the Promise was typical of the genre when it was used in general situations of war and not when it was employed before an imminent battle.

[3]For a discussion of the history of research on this subject see E. W. Nicholson, *Preaching to the Exiles* (Oxford: Blackwell, 1970) 20-32.

[4]See O. Kaiser, *Isaiah 1-12* (Old Testament Library; Philadelphia: Westminster, 1972) 90. He says the following concerning Isaiah's meeting with Ahaz "The prophet is sent here to meet the king, not of course because Ahaz would not have received him in his palace on the pretext of urgent government business, but because of the profound symbolism inherent in the whole scene. Care for an adequate water supply in case of siege was one of the most important defensive tasks of the king, for it was a particularly

weak point . . . The king, who sought to save himself by his own actions, was inspecting the vital water supply for this purpose, and was no doubt taking steps to increase it on this occasion by new arrangement. At this very point he is directed towards God, who alone is capable of giving and sustaining."

[5]See, e.g., Kaiser, *Isaiah 1-12*, 87.

[6]See the discussion of this pericope in Chp. I.

[7]It is probable that the extended length of this element is due to the redactional activity. See Kaiser, *Isaiah 1-12*, 94.

[8]Ibid.

[9]For a discussion of the prophets Jeremiah and Isaiah and their links to their respective traditions see R. R. Wilson, *Prophecy and Society in Ancient Israel* (Philadelphia: Fortress, 1980) 231ff. and 270ff.

[10]The texts to which we will refer have often been understood to support the thesis that the "fear not" oracles in Second Isaiah are Oracles of Salvation. See, for example, P. B. Harner, "The Salvation Oracle in Second Isaiah," JBL 88 (1969) 418-35 and A. Schoors, *I Am God Your Saviour* VTSup 24 (Leiden: Brill, 1973) 34-36.

[11]Our discussion is dependent on the translation of Franz Rosenthal, ANET, 655-56. The text also appears in AOT, 443-44.

[12]ANET, 655.

[13]R. H. Pfeiffer dates the oracle in 667 B.C.E. at the beginning of Ashurbanipal's reign (ANET, 451). Here we are following his translation.

[14]See Appendix II.

[15]See Chps. V, VI and VII.

[16]This is true of the Deuteronomic History where the genre is employed by Yahweh to give orders to Moses and Joshua.

[17]See Chp. V.

[18]Our discussion is dependent on the translation of R. D. Biggs, ANET, 606. An earlier translation by R. H. Pfeiffer also appears in ANET, 451.

[19]ANET, 606, 1.75.

[20]See the discussion of 1 Kgs 6:8-23 in Chp. I.

[21]There is another text addressed to Ashurbanipal that uses the phrase "fear not" (see AOT, 266) and a collection of oracles concerning Esarhaddon (ANET, 449-450; a later translation is found in ANET, 605). In these texts the structure of the oracles is more fluid than in most of the biblical texts. While details of the cultic setting of these oracles are not particularly clear, the oracles generally concern the protection of the king against his enemies and/or the deity's promise to maintain the king in his office. We will refer later to the oracles addressed to Esarhaddon in our discussion of the "fear not" oracles in Second Isaiah and in Genesis.

CHAPTER IV: THE TEMPLE AS CITADEL

[1]This text is sometimes cited as an example of the Priestly Oracle of Salvation in response to the lament of Jehoshaphat (vss. 5-12). See A. Schoors, *I Am God Your Saviour*, VTSup 24 (Leiden: Brill, 1973) 34. However, the fact that the words are addressed to the community and not the individual has required some explanation since

the so-called *Heilsorakel* is usually understood to have been addressed to an individual. Furthermore, the use of the prophetic messenger formula in vs. 15 has also required some explanation since the *Heilsorakel* is usually understood as a priestly and not a prophetic form of speech.

[2]See the discussion of these texts in Chp. III.

[3]See above pp. 60-61.

[4]This phrase is close to the phrase used in Isa 41:8. See below pp. 89-90.

[5]The phrase is used in a similar way in Isa 43:1 and 44:1. See below pp. 92-93.

CHAPTER V: THE COMMUNITY AS KING IN SECOND ISAIAH

[1]For example, this is the view of Claus Westermann. See his "Das Heilswort bei Deuterojesaja," EvT 24 (1964) 359; "Sprache und Struktur der Prophetie Deuterojesajas" *Forschung am Alten Testament* (TBü 24; München: Chr. Kaiser, 1964) 118 and *Isaiah 40-66* (The Old Testament Library; Philadelphia: Westminster, 1969) 11. A significant aspect of Westermann's form critical work on Second Isaiah was that he restricted the number of occurrences of the so-called Oracles of Salvation in Second Isaiah to these five or six texts. (In the two articles, although not in the commentary, he lists 54:4-6 in brackets as a possible representative of the *Gattung*.) Begrich in his *Studien zu Deuterojesaja* ([Bwant 77; Stuttgart: Kohlhammer, 1938]; reprinted in [TBü 20; München: Chr. Kaiser Verlag, 1963]) claimed that there were 24 examples of the *Heilsorakel* in Second Isaiah (pp. 14-26). It was Westermann's contention that Begrich had confused two *Gattungen*, both related to lament: the *Heilsorakel*, a priestly form, and the *Heilsankündigung*, a prophetic form of speech. See also A. Schoors, *I Am God Your Saviour* (VTSup 24; Leiden: Brill, 1973), 80-84 who sees these five texts plus 54:4-6 as Oracles of Salvation.
Westermann, unlike Schoors, is somewhat hesitant to understand 54:4-6 as representing the Oracle of Salvation. While 54:4-6 is a "fear not" text, we would also understand that it represents a structure that is somewhat different from that of the five texts that we will treat in this chapter. It has affinities with the oracle addressed to Hagar. See Chp. VII, note 25.

[2]R. P. Merendino has noted the similarity between the so-called *Heilsorakel* in Second Isaiah and Josh 10:8. He says, "Interessant ist ferner ein Vergleich mit Jos 10,8. Diese Stelle weist die ähnliche formale Struktur wie unsere deuterojesajanischen Texte auf: Aufforderung im Imperativ (fürchte dich nicht), Begründung im Perfekt (ich gebe sie in deine Hand) und Folge im Imperfekt (niemand unter ihnen wird vor dir standhalten können). Sie ist freilich die einzige Stelle, die der Struktur nach den Texten Jes 41,8-13.14-16; 43:1,4.5-7; 44,1-4 gleicht." *Der Erste und der Letzte: Eine Untersuchung von Jes 40-48* (VTSup 31; Leiden, 1981), 165. See also his "Literarkritisches, Gattungs-kritisches und Exegetisches zu Jes. 41,8-16," *Bib* 53 (1972) 25ff.

[3]The thesis of this chapter differs from the thesis of my article, "Fear Not Oracles in Second Isaiah," VT (1984) 129-52. In the article I suggested that the two "fear not" oracles in Isa 41 represented a genre which was related to War Oracles in the Deuteronomic History while the "fear not" oracles in Isa 43 and 44 represented a different genre which was more closely related to "fear not" oracles addressed to the patriarchs in Genesis. I now argue that all the texts represent a single genre, "the language of address to a warrior." The variation in the structure of the text I now understand to be a variation in the structure of the genre when it is used to address a king. Associating the vocation of Jacob/Israel with kingship picks up an observation I made in my dissertation, *Patriarchal Traditions in Second Isaiah* (Princeton Theological Seminary, 1974) 154-67.

[4]See above Chp. III.

[5]I have translated the verbs here which are in the Hebrew perfect tense in the past tense, unlike the RSV which translates them in the future tense.

[6]The Object of Fear does not occur in the extra-biblical occurences of the genre when a king is addressed. See above Chp. III and Appendix II. Indeed, this element is consistently missing in the other proto-apocalyptic literature (See Chp. VI) and in the occurrence of the genre in the Pentateuch (see Chp. VII).

[7]See above p. 65.

[8]The Address regularly occurs in extra-biblical oracles spoken to kings. See Appendix II. It is also important to observe here that an Address frequently occurs when the genre is used to assure a community (see Deut 20:3-4; Hag 2:4-9).

[9]See Deut 20:3-4 and 2 Chr 20:15-17.

[10]See the discussion of Deut 31:1-8 in Chp. I.

[11]It is interesting to note here that the coastlands are afraid when they have seen (ראו); seeing has instilled fear. In our discussion of the conventional language of war we have argued that "seeing" often functioned as a basis for the Assurance, "fear not" (see Josh 8:1-2 and Jer 1:4-19). It is possible here that this "seeing" which produces "fear" among the nations is intended as a contrast to the comforting "fear not" oracles addressed to Jacob/Israel in Isa 41:8ff.

[12]See Appendix II for a discussion of these oracles.

[13]See p. 154.

[14]See pp. 155-56.

[15]See Yehoshua Gitay, *Prophecy and Persuasion: A Study of Isaiah 40-48* (Forum Theologiae Linguisticae 14; Bonn: Linguistica Biblica, 1981) 63-76.

[16]RSV translates אתן "I give."

[17]תולעת is used in the sense of insignificance in Job 25:6 and Psalm 27:7. The meaning of מתי is more difficult. The suggestion of Driver that it is related to the Accadian *mutu* meaning "louse" in "Linguistic and Textual Problems: Isaiah XL - LXVI," JTS 36 (1935) 399 is unlikely since *mutu* does not occur in Accadian in the sense that Driver suggests. The form *mutu* meaning "louse" is not found either in *The Assyrian Dictionary* (ed. A. L. Oppenheim et al.; Chicago: Oriental Institute, 1977), vol. 10, pp. 313-319 or in B. Meissner and W. von Soden, *Akkadisches Handwörterbuch* (Weisbaden: Harrasowitz, 1967) vol. 8, p. 691. In the Old Testament מתי occurs with מספר (Gen 34:30; Deut 4:27, 33:6; Jer 44:28; Ps 105:12//1 Chr 16:19) and with מעט (Deut 26:5, 28:62) meaning "few." It is possible that מתי can carry the meaning of "few" apart from its association with either מספר or מעט. The LXX translates ολιγοστος ("few").

[18]See O. Schilling, "בשר, bŝr, בשורה," TDOT (ed. G. Johannes Botterweck and Helmer Ringgren; Grand Rapids: Eerdmans, 1975), vol. 2, p. 315.

[19]See, for example, Isa 17:13 and 29:5. Also see C. Westermann, *Isaiah 40-66*, 77 who interprets the language this way.

[20]See J. Muilenburg, "The Book of Isaiah: Chapters 40-66," IB 6 (ed. G. Buttrick; New York: Abingdon, 1956) 459; and C. Westermann, *Isaiah 40-66*, 77. The word "mountain" is used similarly in Zech 4:7 to refer to the obstacles facing Zerubbabel who has the responsibility of completing the building of the temple. Before Zerubbabel the mountain of obstacles will become a plain (מישר). See P. R. Ackroyd (*Exile and Restoration* [London: SCM, 1968] 173) who understands "mountain" in Zech 4:7 in this way. Furthermore, the notion that these obstacles will be moved by the spirit of Yahweh and not by the power and might of Zerubbabel is related to the vocation of Jacob/Israel who is not a mighty warrior but a "herald of good tidings" announcing Yahweh's victory. Our contention is opposed to that of E. J. Hamlin ("The Meaning of 'Mountains and Hills' in Isa 41:14-16," JNES 13 [1954] 189) who understands "mountains and hills" to refer to "sanctuaries," "altars" and "images" to be destroyed by Israel in the new conquest of the

land. That interpretation fails to take into account that Israel's warfare is ended and that, while Israel is addressed as a warrior, her vocation is not that of the typical warrior wielding destruction but as the herald announcing Yahweh's victory.

[21] Both the verbs גיל and הלל are used in the book of Isaiah in contexts associated with the celebration at the end of the war. In Isa 40:26 the *qal* of גיל is used to express rejoicing that accompanies the dividing of spoils of war and in 45:25 the *hithpael* of הלל is used to speak about glorying in the triumph over enemies.

[22] See my *Patriarchal Traditions in Second Isaiah*, 119ff.

[23] See C. Westermann, *Isaiah 40-66*, 70-71.

[24] C. Westermann suggests that the designations of the servant are related to royalty (ibid., 94-95).

[25] See note 3.

[26] Form critics who interpreted these texts as Oracles of Salvation understood ועתה not as a clue to context but as an indication of the *Sitz im Leben* where the Oracle of Salvation supposedly represented an answer to and reversal of the preceding lament. See A. Schoors, *I Am God Your Saviour*, 68. Failure to see that ועתה is an important indication of *Sitz im Text* resulted in part from an incorrect identification of the genre.

[27] See C. Westermann, *Isaiah 40-66*, 17 and A. Schoors, *I Am God Your Saviour*, 189-97 and 201-7.

[28] See C. Westermann, *Isaiah 40-66*, 109 who links these two trial speeches with the disputation in Isa 40:27-31.

[29] Following the RSV, although commentators have found these difficulties with the text: (1) עבדי in 42:19a is translated in the plural by the versions, a reading of the text followed by some critics, (2) 42:19b is translated by the Vulgate as *nisi ad quem nuncios meos misi*, "as he to whom I have sent my messengers," an apparent paraphrase of the Hebrew which is nevertheless adopted by some scholars; (3) 42:19cd appears to be a repetition of 42:19ab which is sometimes seen as evidence of textual corruption of the original; and (4) the meaning of משלם in 42:19d is not clear and has received a variety of translations.

[30] C. Westermann, *Isaiah 40-66*, 109.

[31] See O. Eissfeldt, "The Promises of Grace to David in Isaiah 55:1-5," *Israel's Prophetic Heritage* (eds. B. W. Anderson and W. Harrelson; New York: Harper and Brothers, 1962) 196-207.

[32] See above Chp. II.

[33] See Appendix II.

[34] ANET, 605.

[35] Ibid.

[36] Ibid., 451.

[37] Ibid., 605.

[38] See, e.g., C. Westermann, *Isaiah 40-66*, 133.

[39] As we will argue in Chp. VII, the promise of offspring (זרע) in Gen 15:1-6 is given in conjunction with a War Oracle, Gen 15:1.

[40]The use of the singular suffix here indicates that Second Isaiah has the patriarch Jacob in mind.

[41]Following the RSV although the last colon is obscure.

[42]See B. W. Anderson, "Exodus Typology in Second Isaiah," *Israel's Prophetic Heritage*, 177-95.

CHAPTER VI: PROTO-APOCALYPTIC ESCHATOLOGY AND THE ANCESTRAL PROMISE

[1]It should also be noted that Jer 30:10-11 does not appear in the LXX. Yet we would argue that when it is understood as a War Oracle, it fits the *Sitz im Text* of Jer 30.

[2]Many form critics have understood the adversative waw in so-called Oracles of Salvation to be a feature of the genre that introduces a response to an hypothesized preceding lament; and the lament is seen as the *Sitz im Leben* of the genre. The adversative waw is rather, according to my argument, a clue to the present setting of the genre in its literary context, its *Sitz im Text*. See Chp. V, note 26.

[3]See J. Bright. *Jeremiah* (AB 21; New York: Doubleday, 1965) 285.

[4]Ibid, 279 and 285-86.

[5]G. Fohrer. *Introduction to the Old Testament* (New York: Abingdon, 1965), 457.

[6]See Isa 40:9-11.

[7]The Hebrew is obscure. Here RSV follows LXX ως εν ημερα εορτης and reads כ׳ום מעד.

[8]It is not a passage concerning the restoration of the messianic king as, for example, Zech 9:9-10.

[9]The community is also referred to as Israel in Zeph 3:14.

[10]See above Chp. V.

[11]See Chps. III and IV.

[12]Fohrer, *Introduction,* 365-73. See also O. Kaiser, *Isaiah 1-12* (Old Testament Library; Philadelphia: Westminster, 1972) 148-49.

[13]There are four other texts which, though the genre appears in them, if at all, only in rudimentary form, have affinities with the War Oracles in Second Isaiah and the oracles in Jeremiah, Zephaniah and Isaiah discussed in this chapter. (1) In Isa 35:4 there is an Encouragement, "be strong" (חזקו) and an Assurance, "fear not" (אל תיראו). Whether these elements should be taken as evidence of a War Oracle is not clear. The context however, has similarities to Second Isaiah. The words which follow the Encouragement and Assurance in vs. 4 are:

> Behold (הבה) your God
> will come with vengeance,
> with the recompense of God.
> He will come and save you.

They resemble the pericope that follows the first occurence of "fear not" in Second Isaiah (Isa 40:9),

> Behold (הנה) the Lord GOD comes
> with might,
> and his arm rules for him,

behold (הנה), his reward is with him,
and his recompense before him.

—Isa 40:10

It has often been observed that this chapter is closely related to Second Isaiah, particularly the prologue (40:1-12) [See e.g., Kaiser, *Isaiah 13-39*, 361-66]. Here we simply note that these two elements of the War Oracle occur in a context similar to that of Second Isaiah's proclamation of the victorious triumph of Yahweh. (2) Jer 10:5b contains an Assurance, "be not afraid" (אל תיראו), an Object of Fear, "of them" (מהם), and a Basis of Assurance "for they cannot do evil/neither is it in them to do good" (כי לא ירעו וגם היטיב אין אותם). The setting concerns the idols which the nations are building (Jer 10:1-5a); Israel is not to fear these idols because they cannot be compared to Yahweh—there is none like him (Jer 10:6-10). While it is not clear that these rudimentary elements should be understood as a War Oracle, the *Sitz im Text* is similar to that of Isa 41:8-16 in which Israel receives War Oracles from Yahweh, in contrast to the nations who are building idols. (3) Elements of the War Oracle may also be evident in Zech 8:13, 15. An Assurance "fear not" (אל תיראו) occurs in both vs. 13 and vs. 15, and the phrase "let your hands be strong" (תחזקנה ידיכם) in vs. 13 is similar to an Encouragement. The context of these words is similar to that of the War Oracles in Isa 43:1-7 and 44:1-5. Yahweh promises the restoration of the community, reversing his former judgment of his people (8:14). (4) Finally Joel 2:21 and 22 contain elements that are related to the War Oracle. The chapter begins by describing how a plague of locusts, like an invading army, has devastated the land (2:1-16). This devastation is understood as a judgment by Yahweh. In response to the intercession of the priests and ministers of Yahweh (2:17), Yahweh says that he has become jealous for his land (2:18) and will rid the land of the invaders (2:20). He then addresses "the land" and "the beasts of the field" as if each were a threatened warrior (2:21-22).

(a)   ASSURANCE
      Fear not,
      אל תיראי

(b)   ADDRESS
      O land,
      אדמה

(c)   DIRECTIVE
      be glad and rejoice
      גילי ושמחי

(d)   BASIS OF ASSURANCE
      for the LORD has done great things!
      כי הגדיל יהוה לעשות

(e)   ASSURANCE
      Fear not,
      אל תיראו

(f)   ADDRESS
      you beasts of the field,
      בהמום שדי

(g)   BASIS OF ASSURANCE
      for the pastures of the
         wilderness are green;
      the tree bears its fruit;
         the fig tree and vine
         give their full yield.
      כי דשאו נאות מדבר
      כי עץ נשא פריו
      תאנה וגפן נתנו חילם

Here the land is to rejoice over the victory of Yahweh. Similarly in Isa 40:9 and Zeph 3:14-16, Zion/Jerusalem is to celebrate Yahweh's victory. In Joel 2:23 the "sons of Zion" are commanded to join in the rejoicing by the land and the beasts of the field.

These four texts, then, contain elements of the War Oracle and have textual settings similar to those in Second Isaiah (discussed in Chp. V) and to those in Jeremiah, Zephaniah and Isaiah considered in this chapter.

CHAPTER VII: THE PATRIARCHAL PROMISE AND THE WAGING OF PEACE

[1]See note in BHS.

[2]O. Kaiser, "Traditionsgeschichte Untersuchung von Genesis 15," ZAW 70 (1958) 113. In this article, Kaiser understands the oracle as a *Heilsorakel* building on the thesis of J. Begrich (see p. 111). While he notes the war ideology of the word "shield," he does not think the oracle should be understood as relating to the military character of Abraham in Gen 14 (see p. 113).

[3]See P. D. Miller, *The Divine Warrior in Early Israel* (Cambridge: Harvard University, 1973) 84-86.

[4]The designation of the deity as the "shield" of the community is found in other psalms, e.g., 59:12. Ps 115 is a liturgy contrasting the power of Yahweh to the powerlessness of the idols. The refrain עזרם ומגנם הוא occurs in vss. 9, 10 and 11.

[5]There are other psalms where the deity, designated as shield, delivers the king from his enemies. In Ps 3:2 the king complains to Yahweh, "How many are my foes (צרי)?" However, he expresses confidence in Yahweh in vs. 4 when he says "But thou, O LORD, art a shield about me" (ואתה יהוה מגן בעדי). This confidence leads the king to say "I am not afraid" (לא אירא), vs. 7. This psalm then picks up two of the motifs of the Genesis oracle but puts them in the mouth of the person addressed rather than in the mouth of the deity. In Gen 15:1 Yahweh says, אל תירא אברם אנכי מגן לך ; here the king says אֹרה יהוה מגן בעדי and confesses לא אירא. Ps 35 contains a similar petition of the king for deliverance from his enemies. He asks Yahweh in vs. 1 to contend (ריב) with those who contend with him and to fight (לחם) with those who fight with him. He does not call Yahweh a מגן here but asks Yahweh to take his implements of war (including his מגן) against those who pursue the petitioner (vs. 2-3). In a similar psalm petitioning for deliverance from enemies and filled with language suggestive of Yahweh's military prowess, the king expresses trust in God when he says "my shield (מגני) is with God who saves the upright in heart" (Ps 7:11). See also Ps 28:7.

[6]See Appendix II, Oracle #4.

[7]In certain passages Yahweh is designated as "shield" when the military associations of the language have receded. See Prov 2:7, 19; 30:5 and Ps 119:14. The fact that "shield" occurs in a War Oracle in Gen 15:1b, however, indicates that the military connotations of the word are important.

[8]See Kaiser, "Traditionsgeschichte Untersuchung," 115 and J. van Seters, *Abraham in History and Tradition* (New Haven: Yale University, 1975) 254.

[9]See van Seters, *Abraham*, 253.

[10]Ibid.

[11]Some scholars have understood the phrase "fear not" as a phrase peculiar to theophany, occurring here to quell the fear experienced upon manifestation of the deity in a vision. See, e.g., the early study of Ludwig Köhler, "Die Offenbarungsformel 'Fürchte dich nicht!' im Alten Testament," *Schweizerische Theologische Zeitschrift* 36 (1919) 33-39. However, many other scholars have argued that "fear not" does not function here or anywhere else in Genesis to alleviate the fear arising from the numinous appearance of the deity. See J. Becker (*Gottesfurcht im Alten Testament* [An Bib 25; Rom: Päpstliches Bibelinstitut, 1965] 53) who says,

> An diesen Stellen (i.e., Gen. 15,1; 21,17; 26,24; 28,13 LXX; and 46,3) ist *'al-tīrā* nicht auf numinose Furcht zu beziehen, sondern dient als

Beruhigungsformel im Hinblick auf eine bestimmte Notlage der
Beteiligten. Ja, es will uns scheinen, dass die betreffenden Perikopen
unter dem Einfluss der literarischen Form des Heilsorakels geprägt
sind; 'al-tîrā hat also dort die Funktion, die ihm im Heilsorakel
zukommt. In Gn. 15,1; 26,24; und 46,3 findet sich zusammen mit 'al-
tîrā auch die charakteristische Ich-Pradikation des Heilsorakels.

Most form critics have also understood the phrase "fear not" in Gen 15:1b to indicate the
Heilsorakel. See H. M. Dion, "The Patriarchal Traditions and the Literary Form of the
Oracle of Salvation!" CBQ 29 (1967) 198-206, and his "The 'Fear Not' Formula and Holy
War," CBQ 32 (1970) 565-70. See also van Seters, *Abraham,* 254. It is our contention
that "fear not" occurs only infrequently in the Hebrew Scriptures to alleviate the fear
caused by the numinous appearance of the deity. See the Introduction, note 3.

[12]See above Chp. III.

[13]The verb, מגן , is used only three times in the Hebrew Scriptures (Gen 14:20; Prov
4:9 and Hos 11:8) and always occurs in the Piel. That the word should be translated
"delivered" or "given" is suggested by its occurrence in Hos 11:8 where it is used in
parallelism with נתן.

[14]For many of these observations of rhetorical links between Gen 14 and 15 I am
indebted to the brief but insightful study of these chapters by N. M. Sarna, *Understanding
Genesis* (New York: Schocken Books, 1966) 121-23. There he notes the relationship of
מגן in Gen 15:1 with מגן in Gen 14:20 and the thematic unity between Yahweh's promise
of שכר and Abram's refusal of רכש. He also notes that while Abram refused רכש, Yahweh
promises רכש to the זרע of Abram in 15:14. He adds,

> The mention of Damascus is another point of contact between the
> two narratives (Gen. 14:15; 15:2), as is the word *berit.* Previously,
> reference was made to Abraham's allies, called in the Hebrew *ba'alei
> berit* (14:13), now God Himself becomes an ally of the patriarch by
> making a covenant *(berit* 15:18) with him. Twice the Amorites are
> mentioned in the story of the 'battle of the kings,' and twice they
> appear in our chapter (vv. 16,21).
> Finally there is every likelihood that Abraham's campaign in which
> a small group prevailed against powerful military opponents is to be
> understood as signaling the fortunes of the patriarch's descendants
> against the formidable enemies listed in the last three verses of the
> chapter.

[15]The situation is similar to that of Jehoshaphat and the people of Judah who
received a War Oracle (2 Chr 20:15-17) in which they were ordered not to fight but who
claimed the booty (רכוש), 2 Chr 20:24ff.

[16]Many form critics who understand Gen 15:16 as a *Heilsorakel* are forced to explain
why Abraham's lament in Gen 15:2-3 follows it. The *Heilsorakel* is supposedly an answer
to lament rather than a form which gives rise to lament. See, e.g., van Seters, *Abraham,*
255-56 who says,

> The real problem with the lament of vv. 2-3 is how to understand its
> form-critical relationship to the salvation oracle of v.1b. One would
> expect the reverse of the order here present, a lament-salvation
> oracle.

[17]Note that Yahweh's answer to Abram's lament in vs. 4 employs the same language
as Yahweh's promise of a dynasty to David in 2 Sam 7:12. In both cases the concern is
for "offspring" (זרע) "who will come from your body" (אשר יצא ממעיך). See van Seters,
Abraham, 255, who points out this similarity.

[18]See, for example, R. Clements, *Abraham and David: Genesis 15 and its Meaning
for Israelite Tradition* (SBT 2/5; London: SCM, 1967).

[19]Many recent studies are beginning to note the connection between the Pentateuch in its final form and its function as an exilic document. See D. J. A. Clines, *The Theme of the Pentateuch* (JSOT Sup 10; Sheffield: JSOT, 1978) 97-100.

[20]See above Chp. IV.

[21]See, e.g., C. Westermann, *The Promises to the Fathers* (Philadelphia: Fortress, 1980) 123.

[22]See Appendix II.

[23]See Appendix II.

[24]See, e.g., BHS, RSV, JB and NAB.

[25]The phrase, אל תיראי, occurs in Isa 54:4-6. While the structure of the War Oracle is difficult to find here, it is possible that the oracle is used here to comfort Zion, the barren one, in contexts similar to those in which Hagar and Esarhaddon's mother was comforted. Yahweh will not only protect the offspring of the "Queen mother" Zion; he will also cause the barren mother to have an abundant offspring.

[26]The LXX has the phrase μη φοβου in 28:13 which occurs in Jacob's dream at Bethel. With the inclusion of this phrase, Gen 28:13-15 could be outlined as a War Oracle as follows:

(a)   SELF-DESIGNATION OF THE DEITY
      I am the LORD, the God of Abraham your father and the God of Isaac,
      אני יהוה אלהי אברהם אביך ואלהי יצחק

(b)   ASSURANCE
      fear not (LXX);
      μη φοβου

(c)   PROMISE
      the land on which you lie I will give to you and to your descendants; and your descendants shall be like the dust of the earth, and you shall spread abroad to the west and to the east and to the north and to the south; and by you and your descendants shall all the families of the earth bless themselves.
      הארץ אשר אתה שכב עליה לך אתננה ולזרעך והיה זרעך כעפר הארץ ופרצת ימה
      וקדמה וצפנה ונגבה ונברכו בך כל משפחת האדמה ובזרעך

(d)   BASIS OF ASSURANCE
      Behold, I am with you.
      והנה א נכי עמך

(e)   PROMISE
      and will bring you back to this land; for I will not leave you until I have done that of which I have spoken to you.
      ושמרתיך בכל אשר תלך והשבתיך אל האדמה הזאת כי לא אעזבך עד אשר אם
      עשיתי את אשר דברתי לך

The occasion of this oracle is an oracular dream like that of Ashurbanipal. It would serve as an oracle offering Jacob protection before returning home to the "enemy," Esau, his brother. It would also help explain the vow Jacob makes in vss. 20-22. Yahweh will be his God, if Yahweh wages "peace" for him (see vs. 21).

[27]See Appendix II where this element is characteristically used in oracles delivered to Esarhaddon.

[28]In this connection see M. Rose, "Entmilitarisierung des Krieges? (Erwägungen zu den Patriarchen-Erzahlungen der Genesis)," BZ 20 (1976) 161-79. In the article he argues that the patriarchal narratives have been demilitarized at the time of the destruction of the state.

CHAPTER VIII: THE WAR ORACLE AND THE ROYAL COMMUNITY IN THE BOOK OF EXODUS

[1]See above Chp. III.

[2]See above Chp. IV.

[3]A second sentence in the Basis of Assurance begins with כי which is also typical of this element.

[4]Compare this oracle also with the oracle in 2 Chr 20:15-17 addressed to King Jehoshaphat and the community.

[5]Also used in the Directive in 2 Chr 20:15-17.

[6]See also 1 Sam 17:16 and Ps 2:2.

CONCLUSION

[1]Philip B. Harner, "The Salvation Oracle in Second Isaiah," JBL 88 (1969) 421-22.

APPENDIX I: THE CALL OF EZEKIEL

[1]The phrases לא תירא and לא תחת also occur in Ezek 3:9. Each of these assurances occurs with an Object of Fear, and a Basis of Assurance also occurs. We will not consider this verse in detail for our explanation of this verse, which is related to the stereotypical language of address to a warrior, would be the same as our explanation of Ezek 2:6-7.

[2]Ezekiel 1 (trans. by Ronald E. Clements; Hermeneia; Philadelphia: Fortress Press, 1979), 44.

[3]Ibid.

[4]Ibid.

[5]Ibid., 106.

[6]It is strange that, if Ezekiel himself were responsible for the call narrative, he would not have been familiar with this genre; Second Isaiah, who was a near contemporary of Ezekiel in Babylon, knew it.

[7]Zimmerli, Ezekiel 1, 46.

APPENDIX II: "FEAR NOT" ORACLES ADDRESSED TO ESARHADDON AND ASHUR-BANIPAL

[1]These texts as well as the three extra-biblical texts discussed in Chp. III have been treated by P. B. Harner in an article, "The Salvation Oracle in Second Isaiah," JBL 88 (1969) 418-35. In the article Harner argued that these extra-biblical texts confirmed the thesis originating with J. Begrich that the "fear not" texts in Second Isaiah should be understood as Oracles of Salvation.

There is another text addressed to Ashurbanipal ("Gebet des Königs Assurbânipal an Nabû und Antwort des Gottes," AOT, 206) that contains the phrase "fear not." This text is sometimes understood as extra-biblical evidence for the Oracle of Salvation. (See Harner, "The Salvation Oracle," 421). It is true that Nabu does answer the petition of Ashurbanipal one time with words that contain the phrase "fear not." But Nabu does not answer the petition of Ashurbanipal only once; he answers him four times, and only once does Nabu use the phrase "fear not." If "fear not" is typical of the so-called Oracle of Salvation, why doesn't it occur in the other three answers to petition? It is important to observe that, when Nabu does address Ashurbanipal with words containing the phrase, "fear not," he is responding especially to Ashurbanipal's petition that Nabu not forget him in the midst of his enemies (". . . , starker Nabu, verlasse mich nicht inmitten meiner Feinde.")

[2] In this discussion the oracles are treated in translation.

[3] I am following the translation of R. D. Biggs, ANET, 605. An earlier translation by R. H. Pfeiffer can also be found in ANET, 449-50.

[4] See P. B. Harner, "The Salvation Oracle," 422 and 426 where he associates these extra-biblical "fear not" texts with war.

[5] See our discussion in Chps. III, V, VI and VII. These features of the structure are also characteristic of the genre when it is used in contexts concerned with warfare in general. (See our discussion of Deut 20:3-4 in Chp. II.)

[6] These features of the genre have their closest parallels in Second Isaiah. See Chp. V.

[7] Harner ("The Salvation Oracle," 421) suggests the possibility of these Esarhaddon texts as well as the "fear not" texts addressed to Ashurbanipal and Zakir (see Chp. III) contain an oracular pattern which appears in a "slightly modified form" in the New Year's Festival at Babylon where the king is assured with the words, "Fear not . . . ! For (?) Bel has spoken . . . , Bel [will hear] your prayer . . . , He will make great your rule . . . , He will exalt your kingdom . . ." (ANET, 334). We would argue that the language of address to a warrior cannot be restricted to any one *Sitz im Leben*. The language is typical of reassurance offered to someone faced with a situation of war generally. The language is modified by the specific context in which it is used—whether that context is an institutional setting, as it may have been in the case of the Esarhaddon oracles, or a purely literary setting, as it is in Second Isaiah.

GENERAL INDEX

Abiathar, 33

Abimelech, 133

Abishai, 26

Abraham, 53, 69, 78-79, 89, 102-103, 105-106, 123, 124, 144, 149, 159

Abram, 127-139

Absalom, 17-19, 26

Ackroyd, P.R., 165 n20

Ahaz, 67, 85, 128, 162 n4

Ahaz, Isaiah's oracle to, 29, 52-63, 79, 121, 131

Ahaziah, 30-31

Ahuzzath, 134

Ammonites, 26, 67, 69

Amnon, 17-19, 26

Amorites, 10, 23

Amphictyony, 1-2, see also Twelve Tribe League

Anderson, B.W., 167 n42

Anderson, G.W., 160 n8

Ashurbanipal, 58-62, 67-68, 100, 128, 133, 163 n13, 163 n21, 171 n26

Ashurbanipal, oracles addressed to, 153-159

Assyria, 28, 64, 129

Assyrians, 120-122

Baal-zebub, 30

Babylon, 49, 97, 104

Babylonia, 50

Babylonians, rule of, 19

Baia of Arbela, 155-156

Barak, 33

Barhadad, 56

Be'elshamayn, 57, 60

Becker, J., 160 n3, 169 n11

Beersheba, 140

Begrich, J., 1, 164 n1, 169 n2, 172 n1

Belet, 154

Belit-abisha, 157-158

Berridge, J.M., 161 n4, 162 n12, 162 n13

Biggs, R.D., 163 n18, 173 n2

Bright, J., 162 n10, 167 n3

Carroll, R.P., 47

Chaldeans, 19

Chronicler's History, 63-79, 147

Clements, R.E., 170 n18, 172 n2

Clines, D.J.A., 171 n19

Community as king, 59, 79-107, 117, 124, 144, see also Royal community

Conquest, 23, 89

Covenant, 55

Covenant, between David and Jonathan, 22

Covenant, with Abram, 131

Covenant, with David, 99, 131

Cross, F.M., 160 n2

Cyrus, 84, 86, 93, 96, 106-107, 123, 129

David, 20-22, 26, 33-34, 53, 72, 99-100

David, address to Mephibosheth, 20-22

David, addresses Solomon, 70-72, 74

Davidic king, 113

Davidic kingdom, 17

Deuteronomic History, 2-4, 6-39, 52, 55-56, 129, 143, 162 n2, 163 n16, 164 n3

Dion, H.M., 170 n11